To Be a Pilgrim

The Medieval Pilgrimage Experience

Sarah Hopper

SUTTON PUBLISHING

First published in 2002 by
Sutton Publishing Limited · Phoenix Mill
Thrupp · Stroud · Gloucestershire · GL5 2BU

British Library Cataloguing in Publication Data
A catalogue record for this book is available from the British Library.

ISBN 0-7509-2620-1

Title page: Pewter shell pilgrim badge. *Museum of London*
Opposite: A fifteenth-century stained glass of St James the Great as a pilgrim, St Mary's Church, Marsham, Norfolk. *John Crook*
Chapter opening pages: Pilgrim badge from the Canterbury shrine of Thomas Becket, mid-late fourteenth century. *Museum of London*

Typeset in 11/13pt New Baskerville.
Typesetting and origination by
Sutton Publishing Limited.
Printed and bound in England by
J.H. Haynes & Co. Ltd, Sparkford.

To Mum, Dad, Ben and Guy,
and in fond memory of
two special souls,
Nanna and Tom.

KL Auril

	g		Saint uliei
.x.		℟.	L egypcienne
.xix.	b	℟.	S. pancrace
.viij.	c	℟.	S. ambroise
	d	℟.	Saint yrame
.xvi.	e	℟.	S. tymothe
.v.	f	℟.	S. machaire
	g	id.	S. apollinaire
.xiii.		id.	Saint proroe
.ij.	b	id.	Saint profere
	c	id.	Saint leon
.x.	d	id.	Saint marcel
	e	id.	S. valerien
.xviij.	f	id.	Saint eufeme
.vij.	g	id.	Saint prime

When you travel, you experience, in a very practical way, the act of rebirth. You confront completely new situations, the day passes more slowly, and on most journeys you don't even understand the language the people speak . . . and you accept any small favour from the gods with great delight, as if it were an episode you would remember for the rest of your life.

Paulo Coehlo, *The Pilgrimage*

St Thomas appears to King Louis VII in a dream, Canterbury Cathedral. *Sonia Halliday Picture Library*

CONTENTS

ACKNOWLEDGEMENTS

I would like to thank those various people who on different levels played an important part in this project. I am grateful to the following for sharing their advice and expertise: Marion Marples at the Confraternity of St James, London; Cressida Annesley, Canterbury Cathedral Archives; Robert Bryden and Rosslyn Chapel, Edinburgh; Richard Eales, University of Kent, Canterbury; The Summer Academy, University of Kent; James Robinson, Medieval and Modern Europe Department at the British Museum; John Clark, Curator of the Early London History and Collections Department at the Museum of London. Thanks also to Professor Martin Biddle, University of Oxford for his initial advice and guidance at the start of the project.

Thanks again to Mum and to Guy for presenting me with two fantastic vestiges of medieval pilgrimage, which in turn inspired new topics for analysis in the writing of this book. Thanks to Sue and Bruno, for the insights that they offered and for providing such comfortable lodgings from which to conduct my research in Rome. I am grateful to those who agreed to cast a discerning eye over the drafts: Dad, Guy, Sue, Bruno, Dr Simon Poulton, Marion Marples and Richard Eales.

Thank you to Mark for keeping saved drafts 'belted, braced and bullet-proof!' To my brother Ben for technical support and his brave, subterranean exploits in Cephalonia; Nick, for taking his camera to Tours; Henry Blagg for the loan of books from Tom's library that assisted in my research.

Thanks must also go to Jane Crompton at Sutton Publishing for offering me a fabulous opportunity which I have relished and to Christopher Feeney, Clare Jackson and Sarah Flight at Sutton for support, guidance and enthusiasm on the way. Thanks to my parents and brother, Ben, for their interest and enthusiasm – here it is! Finally, but not least, to Guy, for unwavering confidence in the success of this endeavour and for sharing its journey.

Within the woodcut:

El padre y madre van a rogar q̃ deſcuelgue el niño viuo.

Como Sanctiago preſeruò el niño ahorcado como ſe ve.

Sancte Iacobe ora pro nobis.

A woodcut of St James the Great in the traditional costume of a pilgrim to Santiago de Compostela. Reproduced in *Folklore y Costumbres de España. Mary Evans Picture Library*

CHAPTER ONE

INSPIRATION AND MOTIVATION FOR PILGRIMAGE

He then set out to visit the shrines of the blessed apostles . . . wishing to spend some of the time of his earthly pilgrimage in the vicinity of holy places, hoping thereby to merit a warmer welcome from the saints in heaven . . . many English people vied with one another in following this custom, both noble and simple, layfolk and clergy, men and women alike.[1]

Pilgrimage held an enduring significance in medieval society up until the sixteenth century, and continues to provoke interest as to its efficacy and its influence on medieval Christianity. Initially encouraged as an act of pious faith, medieval pilgrimage reveals something of the workings of the medieval psyche, as well as the mechanics of society, and the many strands of its subject matter allow the historian a deeper understanding of what moved, motivated and inspired its participants. With the use of contemporary sources, this book aims to offer an introduction to the concepts and practicalities of pilgrimage, as well as the personal experience of the pilgrims themselves.

It seems likely that the popular practice of pilgrimage in Christian history predates its first literary mention. Documentary evidence shows that pilgrims were travelling to the Holy Land as early as the third century. In modern times many people, not just Christians, still go on pilgrimage, and its appearance as a recurrent theme in art, opera, poetry and church hymns testify to its popular and enduring significance. It is a practice that continues to traverse the boundaries of race, religion and class.

Among the notable pilgrims of the twentieth century was Hitler, who journeyed to the tombs of Napoleon Bonaparte and Heinrich I, a tenth-century Saxon warrior. Presumably, he sought the same encouragement and inspiration from his chosen mentors as those medieval pilgrims who sought solace and guidance at the shrines of their favoured saints. Today, writers can seek their muse among the tombs of celebrated authors and poets in Westminster Abbey. Others may take their curiosity or devotion to the birthplace of Shakespeare, the embalmed body of Lenin in Moscow, to Gracelands or to historic battlefields. For some this is an uplifting and inspiring experience, for others humbling and introspective. For the medieval Church,

Fourteenth-century bench end of a pilgrim, Chester Cathedral. *John Crook*

the desired response of the pilgrim was sequentially laid out in the writings of a thirteenth-century German Bishop named Theoderich.

> To bear Christ in remembrance, and by remembering him may learn to love him, by loving may pity him who suffered near these places; through pity, may acquire a longing for him, by longing for him may be absolved from their sins; by absolution from sin may obtain his grace, and by his grace may be made partakers of the kingdom of heaven.[2]

While no easy task, such journeys of faith that took men and women thousands of miles from their homes, often for months at a time, came to be a spontaneous and popular activity within all levels of medieval society. Their aim was to visit the shrine or holy place associated with a particular religious figure, whether it be a venerated saint or the birthplace of Jesus himself. The reward was a place in heaven. Aware of the torments of purgatory and hell, such a journey must also have carried a sense of urgency and obligation for much of medieval society.

The great prestige and spiritual virtuosity of a venerated figure were felt to be most readily experienced by visiting their shrine. This was usually located at the place of their birth or death, and usually heralded as the centre of their cult. Here the pilgrim could more easily attempt to recreate the saint's life and suffering on a meditative level, immersed in the same surroundings that had once been familiar to the departed. Through this process, the pilgrim would also expiate himself of some of his guilt for sins committed.

This notion of a cathartic appeasement of guilt through mental or physical submission was also applied to the journey of pilgrimage itself. In enduring the hardships and dangers of a pilgrimage, it was believed that the pilgrim could alleviate his sins through the experience of suffering, just as Christ had suffered in order to free man of sin before. In this respect, the greater the spiritual and physical endurance the journey presented, the better.

In his record of his journey to the Holy Land in the twelfth century, Saewulf of Canterbury stated that he did not take the direct route by sea with the others, 'whether because of the burden of my sins or because no ship was available'. This seems to imply that by choosing a more prolonged journey, his absolution would be more effective though the ordeals and suffering that might come with it.[3]

> Do you think to escape what no mortal man has been able to escape? Which of the Saints lived without cross or trial? Even our Lord Jesus was never without sorrow and pain as long as He lived.[4]

The word pilgrimage comes from the latin *peregrinatio*, meaning a journey undertaken to a sacred site in devotional spirit. Although the Church's preachings on purgatory and salvation held sober meaning for the medieval conscience, ultimately pilgrimage was still a practice undertaken through personal choice. However, this is in contrast with some other religions. In the Muslim tradition pilgrimage still constitutes an ostensible part of its belief system, as well as an obligatory part of Islamic religious duty. This is not to say though that medieval pilgrimage carried any less weight or significance. Pilgrimage permeated medieval life and society in profound and influential ways, affecting most people's lives either directly or indirectly.

Illustrations from Anton Sorg's second Ausburg edition of *The Travels of Sir John Mandeville*, 1481.

There were those, for example, who endured the long absences of family members on pilgrimage and others whose loved ones never returned. William the Conqueror's father, Robert, Duke of Normandy, lost his life on a pilgrimage to the Holy Land when William was eight years old. There were others whose commercial enterprise meant that they played a vital role in what could fairly be described as the pilgrimage 'industry', such as market vendors, taverners, souvenir sellers, hostel and hospital workers and ship owners.

The poet Dante took the opportunity to classify the different types of pilgrim as he saw them. A pilgrim could be anyone making a pilgrimage away from his native homeland. He cites the most notable of these journeys as that to the shrine of St James in the Galician region of Spain, 'because the burial place of St James was further away from his country than that of any other apostle'. Palmers are specified as those pilgrims who travel overseas, namely on the transmarine voyage to the Holy Land where palm motif tokens were purchased by pilgrims. Lastly, 'romeos are those who go to Rome'. In his annotation of pilgrim types, Dante also underlines the importance of these three destinations as those of the greatest significance to all pilgrims.[5]

The Holy Land, as the location of Jesus's life and death, Rome, as the political centre of the Roman Catholic Church, and Santiago de Compostela, the place of St James's burial, were the top ranking destinations. There were also a host of other shrines to saints liberally scattered across Europe, among those of course, the great Augustinian priory of Canterbury, site of the eponymous murder in the cathedral of Thomas Becket.

While early Christianity focused more on the oral dispersal of the gospel, the marking-out of sacred locations created recognised destination points for the pilgrim that facilitated the increasing popularity of such journeys. The practice of pilgrimage was also underpinned by the popular concept that certain places and sites were favoured by God, and, therefore, had a greater spiritual puissance, or vibe. Equally, the Church's selection and promotion of certain saints further endorsed particular sites. Their magnetism lay in the belief that through visiting them, the pilgrim brought himself closer to God by entering into the presence of his deceased servant.

A similar practice is enacted every twelve years at the festival of the Kumbh Melah in India. In 2001, an estimated 70 million people gathered at the banks of the River Ganges at Allahabad. There are three striking similarities between the practice and belief behind this Hindu festival and Medieval pilgrimage. Foremost is the undertaking of a devotional journey to a marked, venerated site of holy significance.

Secondly, the ritual bathing in the waters of the Ganges is strongly reminiscent of the bathing of medieval pilgrims, for purposes of both spiritual and physical healing. Examples for the medieval pilgrim were the holy pools of Walsingham or St Winifrede's and the practice of bathing in the Lavamentula River before arriving at St James's shrine at Compostela. The idea that the water of these sites held magical, supernatural properties capable of physical healing and spiritual cleansing is common to both. At Canterbury, for example, a minute amount of St Thomas's blood gave healing properties to the Holy Water dispensed to pilgrims there. At the Ganges, it was a drop of holy nectar imparted in its waters by the gods. Medieval pilgrims often purchased ampoules of holy water for consumption or anointing.

Thirdly, timing was of the essence to both. For medieval pilgrims, attending a shrine on the day of a holy festival enhanced the religious experience, charging it with greater divine significance and energy. Many holy shrines also offered greater indulgences or remission from sin on such festivals. Equally, the Kumbh Melah is an event scheduled on a chosen day that witnesses an auspicious astrological conjunction. The results are the same in both cases, with the faithful gathering to partake of the heightened, magical atmosphere.

In an ascetically pious society, that by its very nature fuelled fear and insecurity, the opportunity to appease the soul of sin was taken by many. While on this spiritual quest, the pilgrim would be reminded of the familiar religious concepts that shaped his society's belief systems by way of the sculptures on the religious buildings he visited. Here the incessant struggle between God and Satanic forces, good and evil, pious servant and infidel, were set in stone for all to witness.

Another prevalent idea among religious writers that encouraged spiritual introspection was that man's days on earth were few and numbered.

> Each morning remember that you may not live until evening; and in the evening, do not presume to promise yourself another day.[6]

For some this may have provoked a more urgent need to commend themselves to God through pilgrimage. For others, the more pressing need to make the most of their days on earth, to 'eat, drink and be merry' as it were, may have been the perceived message.

Thomas à Kempis's words also remind us of the ever present dangers and struggles of medieval life, which made for greater hardships and higher mortality rates.

> Foolish man, how can you promise yourself a long life. . . . You have often heard how this man was slain by the sword; another drowned; how another fell from a high place and broke his neck; how another died at table; how another met his end in play.[7]

There existed in medieval text and belief the analogy of life itself as a kind of pilgrimage. It extolled the idea that man's days on earth were in themselves a journey of pilgrimage towards the soul's enlightenment and unity with God.

> What do you seek here since this world is not your resting place? Your true home is in Heaven; therefore remember that all the things of this world are transitory.[8]

In Hebrews 11: 13–16, Paul refers to man's status on earth as that of stranger and pilgrim. Importance is also placed on the notion of enduring this passage on earth in order to secure a better life thereafter, a belief that Bede reiterated in his early writings. Man's existence on earth was temporary and therefore he was to serve it as pious guest before being called away to his next resting place.[9]

To further endorse this notion, Jesus himself is depicted as a pilgrim, such as in the Church of Santo Domingo de Silos on the road to Compostela and biblical stories were recalled to support this, for example the arduous pilgrimage that was the Exodus from Egypt to the Promised Land. Later, in the seventeenth century, John Bunyan's *Pilgrim's Progress*, a tale of a man and his epic spiritual pilgrimage through life with all its tribulations, is another use of the same theme.

Such ideas may seem overtly anachronistic compared to those of modern life. Today progress tends to be measured in terms of technological advancement or groundbreaking discovery rather than piety and purity. Nonetheless, pilgrimage still thrives either as a duty or pious exercise for many religions, as well as being adopted by those of a more secular outlook.

Aside from the main focus of pilgrimage in seeking the union of one's soul to God and paying respect to a venerated religious figure, for many medieval pilgrims such visits also came with the hope of a healing miracle. Documentary evidence lists a significant number of miracle cures divinely dispensed to those arriving at shrines with physical ailments. Such miracles were sometimes recorded on site for posterity; for example, the monks William and Benedict of Canterbury Cathedral listed those miracles profited by St Thomas. Those occurring at St Wulstan's shrine in Worcester were logged in *c.* 1240 as the *Miraculi Sancti Wulstani.*

Also, the Church had the power to grant pardons or 'indulgences' to pilgrims, sold at various shrines. These granted forgiveness for past sins, saving the recipient from a fixed duration in purgatory, whether it be days, months or years. They also relieved the recipient of part or all of a penance. Prior to this, forgiveness could be exchanged for penitential punishment, for example an agreed number of lashes equal to the weight of the sin. However, the sale of indulgences at sacred sites also served as a valuable source of income for the related monastery, whose duties would include maintaining the roads and bridges in its vicinity. However, by 1230 the Church had come to realise that on a spiritual level it was not in a position to measure purgatory in terms of cash sums or punishments.

Further evidence suggests that there may also have been other very different urges and incentives for the medieval pilgrim. In an age when the three things that drove a man from his home were noted by a contemporary writer as 'a quarrelsome wife, a smoking fireplace and a leaking roof'[10] a pilgrimage clearly offered the chance to escape from the banalities of daily routine and take retreat. With this in mind, it is not surprising to note that the Church later challenged the misuse of pilgrimage as a holiday, to visit new lands and experience cultures unknown. Yet aside from escapism, the experience of temporarily forsaking the familiar world for what was as yet uncharted territory for many pilgrims, must also have inspired feelings of great anticipation and emotion. For some, it may also have offered the chance for reflection and re-evaluation on life in a way not normally afforded by domestic routine and rigorous labour.

For the majority, the medieval home consisted of one multi-functional area or hall (in the case of manor houses) in which cooking, eating and sleeping would take place. The appartments of Edward I at the Tower of London were an exception indicative of noble birth; while there was still an 'aula', or hall for eating, entertainment and the knights of the household to sleep in, the king had the privilege of his own bedroom. Medieval society was well accustomed to the reality of communal living and a lack of privacy. Pilgrimage offered a more liberating experience, though not necessarily a solitary one. Large groups of pilgrim bands fulfilled what was undoubtedly a social need for those leaving home. Pilgrimage was a chance to experience some level of freedom from domestic constraints, travelling in company and fellowship.

Another very real aspect of medieval life that may have inspired pilgrimage was the regularity of famine and pestilence. While the upper classes and nobility could afford

Ploughing with oxen from the Luttrell Psalter, fourteenth century. *British Library/Bridgeman Art Library*

Sowing from the Luttrell Psalter. *British Library/Bridgeman Art Library*

Harvesting wheat from the Luttrell Psalter. *British Library/Bridgeman Art Library*

Burial of plague victims in 1349 from the *Annales* of Gilles de Muisit, 1352. *MS 13076–7, f. 24 v, Bibliothèque Royale de Belgique, Brussels/Bridgeman Art Library*

to import food if need be, the majority were at the mercy of the year's harvest. It was not unusual for people to die during the winter months due to sickness or as the victims of a poor crop yield. In such times of trouble the help or forgiveness of God and his saints would often be invoked by undertaking a pilgrimage.

Equally, while references to hygiene in medieval texts are mostly limited to the washing of hands and face, squalid living conditions certainly served to create a breeding ground for disease. An example is the floors of many medieval homes which were normally strewn with rushes. In his recipe for creating a fine plaster, the fourteenth-century Florentine artist Cenino Cennini recommends using the oldest and driest chicken bones that can be found lying about on the floor! Many people would also sleep on the floor at home.

Equally disturbing is Erasmus's description of domestic hygiene in the 1520s. In his letter to Wolsey's physician, he complains of the foul stench in many homes which again he puts down to the irregular changing of floor rushes and their resulting contents: 'spittle and vomit and urine of dogs and men, beer that hath been cast forth and remnants of fishes and other filth unnamable . . . a vapour which in my judgement is far from wholesome for the human body.'[11]

Although the plague was not constantly raging, it seems likely that it was never entirely absent from England. Virulent and pernicious, it had the capacity to flare up spontaneously and without warning. In the belief that such events were a physical manifestation of divine wrath, pilgrimage would be undertaken as a journey of penance, to beg forgiveness, or indeed to give thanks for the preservation of one's life.

In this way, many pilgrimages were also undertaken on the strength of a vow. These may have occurred at a precarious moment in prayer for one's safe passage home, or the preservation of one's life in a storm at sea. The promise would be made that in return a pilgrimage would be undertaken to the invoked saint's shrine. If the person was then unable to make the journey for reasons of illness, frailty or otherwise, papal dispensation would be required in order to commute the vow and make arrangements for it to be satisfied in some other way. This often required the sending of money, gifts or a proxy pilgrim to the shrine in question. In one recorded instance, a French laywoman in the throes of a difficult labour had consented to her husband's vow that they would undertake a pilgrimage if she be delivered safely from childbirth. Later, a request was made for commutation of the wife's vow on account of her thereafter being pregnant every year and therefore unfit for such a journey.[12]

In a similar way, evidence suggests that as for the knight preparing to go to war, pilgrimage held a practical purpose. Before setting out on his mission, the knight would undertake a pilgrimage as a means to securing divine favour. On returning safely from his duties, he would then go on pilgrimage again in thanksgiving for his safe passage home. Richard the Lionheart did just this in the twelfth century. Having been captured by the Duke of Austria in Vienna (his disguise having failed him), he was kept prisoner for seventeen months in Durnstein Castle on the Danube. His ordeal over, he undertook a pilgrimage of thanksgiving to the shrine of St Thomas of Canterbury, for his safe return. He reputedly walked the last leg of the journey from Sandwich barefoot.

Pilgrims would also use their visit to a holy shrine to request assistance in a particular area of their life. It is thought that Henry VIII's unerring devotion to the shrine of Our Lady at Walsingham was concerned with his longing for a male heir. He related to duly visited the shrine again on the occasion of his son Henry's birth in 1511. However, reasons for pilgrimage were not always concerned with life-and-death situations. Louis VII was known for his pilgrimages in request and thanksgiving for ridding himself of bad wives and acquiring new, more favourable ones!

Pilgrimage could also carry penitential significance. Henry II's pilgrimage to the shrine of St Thomas Becket in 1174 was one of self-imposed penance for his knights' murder of the bishop in 1170. Other pilgrims, however, had their penance thrust upon them when they were made to undergo pilgrimage as atonement for a crime. For example, strict penitential measures were laid out by Pecham, Archbishop of Canterbury, in 1283 for a profligate parish priest. His three-year penance for unrepentant 'incontinence and fornication' was to begin with a pilgrimage to the shrine of St James at Compostela. The year following he was to visit the relics of SS Peter and Paul at Rome and in the third year make pilgrimage to Cologne.[13]

The crimes for which pilgrimage was imposed as penitential punishment varied in degree and nature. The pilgrimages appropriated to different crimes by one bishop of Rochester in the fourteenth century also suggest that graded levels of punishment were devised. The most severe was imposed for the incestuous infraction of adultery with a godmother and for this, a pilgrimage to Santiago is prescribed. Adultery and fornication are also dealt with severely with the penance lasting up to six years.[14]

The purpose of such penitential pilgrimage was for the punishment as well as the salvation of transgressors, even for salvation of the soul of their victims if the crime had been murder. As pilgrimage became an increasingly popular practice, though, it was noted that this punishment was rather insubstantial and was being abused, and, therefore, was later abandoned.

For the more cunning still, pilgrimage could be a way of temporarily evading arrest for a crime committed. As a wearer of the sacred cross, the pilgrim's sanctity was assured under the protection of St Peter and the Pope. He became beyond the reach of the 'long arm of the law' (except the ecclesiastical), and could not be arrested or taken to civil court. It seems possible that it was this kind of assurance that led to the existence of the palmer or professional pilgrim who existed on permanent pilgrimage. While on pilgrimage, as with all pilgrims, the criminal would be encouraged to seek forgiveness for his misdeeds.

For those who were too weak, sick or frail to embark on their own pilgrimages, it was possible to employ someone to make the journey on their behalf. Such 'hired pilgrims' would deliver devotions and requests in your name at the shrine of your choosing. Others requested in their will that a pilgrimage should be taken for them in the event of their death. Archbishop of Canterbury, Henry Chichele (1362–1443), had noted that a suitable chaplain should be chosen to do him this honour on his death. The doomed first wife of Henry VIII, Katherine of Aragon, had written a clause in her will requesting that someone make pilgrimage to the shrine at Walsingham to which she had been devoted in her lifetime.

As the popularity of pilgrimage increased, so did its appeal as an excuse for a spring jaunt rather than a religious exercise, thus attracting severe criticism. It became a social adventure with minstrels and dancers following pilgrim bands and providing entertainment. Many more merchants and artisans would join the merriment on their own journeys, enjoying the security and benefits of travelling in a large group. This is the scene most strongly reminiscent of Chaucer's fourteenth-century *Canterbury Tales*, with its bustle of story-telling pilgrims, including corrupt men of holy orders and bawdy simpletons. Here the auspicious and celebrated arrival of spring is projected as the inspiration and backdrop for pilgrimage. It seems an almost pagan celebration of the official close of the winter's harsh duration.

> Whan that Aprill with his shoures soote
> The droghte of March hath perced to the roote . . .
> Thanne longen folk to goon on pilgrimages.[15]

This is not to say, though, that there were not those wayfarers of genuine piety and faith who truly believed in the efficacy of their journey. In the *Canterbury Tales*, it is the Parson that represents this faction, rich in pious thoughts and enduring in hardship.

There are surviving monastic rolls that give a clear idea of the lucrative nature of pilgrimage in terms of the money and offerings received by the various shrines. We also have some surviving records of reported miracles and to whom they occurred. Sadly though, there are fewer accounts of individual pilgrimages, and the evidence we do have is often restricted to the experiences of the wealthy nobility. As one historian has commented, 'pilgrimage was too common to be noted unless linked with the movements of an important person.'[16] This lack of first-hand evidence may also be due to the fact that up until the fourteenth century literacy was confined to the nobility and the Church. However, the lure of pilgrimage reached every level of the social hierarchy.

> both small and great, rich and poor alike draw the water of life; and they who
> freely and willingly serve Me, shall receive grace upon grace.[17]

CHAPTER TWO

SANCTO PASSAGIO TRANSMARINO: PILGRIMAGE TO THE HOLY LAND

Naaman of Syria bathed himself in that river [Jordan] seven times, and he was healed of his leprosy and made sound as a fish.[1]

The Holy Land offered the pilgrim a host of sites traditionally connected with the life and times of the holy family. With God seen as untouchable and omnipotent, the Holy Land offered the medieval visitor a chance to encounter the memory of Jesus: the living, breathing man.

The letters of St Jerome (*c.* 342–420), who settled in Palestine in the fourth century, testify to the great number of visitors who made their way to Jerusalem at this early stage in the history of pilgrimage; he says it was as if the whole of mankind had arrived there at once. The later writings of Theoderich show that this trend continued well into the twelfth century and persisted into the sixteenth century and beyond. He described the sheer weight of pilgrim traffic that vied for space in the chapel of Mount Calvary alone:

Here, at the top of the stairs, stand Guardians watching the gate, who only allow as many pilgrims as they choose to enter, lest by excessive pressure, as often happens, there is crushing or danger to life.[2]

More than any other venerated site, the Holy Land provided an accessible and tangible link with Christ as the place 'where our Lord was quick and dead'.[3] It is for this reason perhaps that pilgrimage to the Holy Land was so highly esteemed and aspired to by pilgrims. Surviving itineraries suggest that pilgrims had begun to travel there in earnest by the fourth century, and its popularity continued to grow. The significance of pilgrimage to the Holy Land is neatly reflected in the 1300 *Mappa Mundi* held in Hereford Cathedral. Here Jerusalem is placed at the centre of the world. In Saewulf's account of his journey to the Holy Land, he cites the place within the walls surrounding the Holy Sepulchre called 'Compas', where Christ measured and marked the centre of the world.

Opposite: Medieval view of Jerusalem. *Ms Fr 9087 f. 85v, Bibliothèque Municipale de Lyon/Bridgeman Art Library*

It was obligatory on arrival at the Jerusalem port of Jaffa to pay for a mule to take you on the rest of your journey. This would not have been a wholly unfamiliar concept to the well-travelled pilgrim, as many of the popular routes, such as London to Canterbury, offered a similar system. It did mean, though, that their free travel now became a more controlled venture. Advice on this situation is given in the fifteenth-century guide book, *Informacion for Pylgrymes*, printed by William Caxton's apprentice Wynken de Worde, using the information of William Wey. 'Also when ye shall take your asse at port Jaffe be not to long behynde your felowes, for and ye come betyme ye may chese the best mule or asse that ye can, for ye shall paye no more for the beest than for the worste.'[4]

Brother Faber[5] also advises the pilgrim not to try to swap the ass, as they are given without the consent of the driver, who would be angered. Pilgrims were then overseen by Muslim officials on their journey towards Jerusalem which included a mandatory stop at the town of Ramla, the Muslim administrative centre for Palestine. Other pilgrims approached Jerusalem from the south through Egypt and Bethlehem, or from Acre in the north.

> And so they went on into the Holy Land until they could see Jerusalem. And when this creature saw Jerusalem – she was riding on an ass – she thanked God with all her heart, praying him for his mercy that just as he had brought her to see this earthly city of Jerusalem, he would grant her grace to see the blissful city of Jerusalem above, the city of Heaven.[6]

Aside from contributing gifts and money, the pilgrim would aspire to receive forgiveness for his sins in the form of 'indulgences'. These were available to pilgrims at nominated shrines offering part remission from punishment in purgatory for sins committed. Superior to these partial indulgences in the pilgrim's eyes were 'plenary indulgences' offering complete remission for all sin. These were first introduced by Pope Urban II in 1095. In exchange a specific pilgrimage was to be made as a crusader to the Holy Land. These

Kneeling Crusader, thirteenth century,
Westminster Psalter, Roy 2 A A XXII f.220.
British Library/Bridgeman

'pilgrims in armour' as they effectively were, fought to free the Holy Land from the grip of the Muslim infidel. Making pilgrimage to Rome during a jubilee year also rewarded the pilgrim with full remission from purgatorial punishment.

Boticcelli's illustrations for Dante's *Purgatory*, the second book of the *Divine Comedy*, offer an insight into why indulgences were such an attractive

Opposite: Mappa Mundi showing Jerusalem as the centre of the Christian world. *British Library/ Bridgeman Art Library*

proposition. Purgatory here is a harrowing depiction of pitiful figures racked with remorse and desperation, sentenced to the torments of their appropriated punishment.

The Holy Land offered several venues which the pilgrim could visit and receive such indulgences, for example the site of the Last Supper on Mount Sion. Most popular were the four hallowed locations within the domed Church of the Holy Sepulchre, namely the Mount of Calvary, the site on which Christ's body was laid after the crucifixion, that where the Holy Cross was buried and most significantly Christ's burial place. Officially, the crucified were denied a formal Jewish burial, but Joseph of Arimathea had requested permission to bury Jesus's body. He placed it within a cave, the mouth of which was then sealed with a rock (Mark 15: 45–7).

Eusebius, in his *Life of Constantine*, describes how these four sites were originally concealed by a Roman temple. Constantine had ordered that the temple's pagan images of wood and stone be cast down and carried away. On removal of the earth, the Holy Sepulchre was exposed beneath the temple's ruins. Constantine was quickly moved to action and ordered that a chapel be built to embrace the sacred marvel. He applied his own private funds as well as State resources to the project, ensuring that these monuments, testament to Christ's existence, were definitively marked out and embellished.

The words of fourteenth-century traveller John Mandeville show the significance that the Holy Sepulchre held for the pilgrim: 'You must understand that when men arrive in Jerusalem, they make their first pilgrimage to the church where is the Sepulchre of our Lord.'[7]

The east face of the Edicule in the Church of the Holy Sepulchre, Jerusalem. *John Crook*

Constantine's fourth-century complex is described by a ninth-century monk as consisting of four chapels whose walls adjoin each other. To the east is a chapel housing Mount Calvary and the place where the cross was unearthed; there is another chapel on the south and a third on the west, in the centre of which the sepulchre stands surrounded by nine columns.[8]

The Holy Sepulchre still represents somewhat of a topographical conundrum for the visitor. At one moment the pilgrim is steered through its network of dimly lit

Opposite: Pilgrims approaching the city gates from *The Travels of Sir John Mandeville* (early fifteenth century). *British Library/Bridgeman Art Library*

passages and at the next plunged into the open space of a chapel. Equally, the coexisting chapels within it occur on differing ground levels, so that the pilgrim must surmount the holy Hill of Golgotha and make descent to the underground rock caves. The tomb sepulchre resides in the heart of the complex.

During a visit to the Holy Land in AD 326 Constantine's mother, the eighty-year-old Empress Helena, is said to have uncovered the True Cross. Three crosses were discovered in all, one of which performed miracles and was thus proven as the cross on which Christ had died. Some of this cross was sent to Constantinople and more found its way to Rome. Today pilgrims can visit the remains of Helena's temple in Rome as well as the Church of Santa Croce, whose later eighteenth-century façade commemorates Helena's ground-breaking archaeological find. The frescoes in the monastery of the Quatro Coronati in Rome also recount the story of the Discovery of the True Cross.

> Saint Helena did not know for certain which was the cross Christ was killed on; so she took each one in turn and laid it on a dead man, and as soon as the True Cross was laid on the dead body, the corpse rose from death to life.[9]

Helena divided her finds into three lots. A section of the *titulus crucis*, or headboard of the cross of Christ, was left in Jerusalem, while another fragment was taken back to Rome. Today, a fragment of walnut wood housed in the Church of Santa Croce in Rome inspires much contemplation among its visitors. Kept close to

A fresco of Helena's discovery of the True Cross, from the Basilica of the Quatro Coronati, Rome.
Sarah Hopper

another intriguing but no less unusual claim for a relic, the finger of Doubting Thomas, the wood fragment is still held by some to be the original *titulus* of Christ's crucifixion. Its letters carry the mocking title, 'Jesus of Nazareth, King of the Jews' in Hebrew, Greek and Latin. Its existence has fuelled enough enquiry to provoke the Vatican's recent consent for its closer scientific analysis. Whether this relic is proven authentic or a fake, it is known from the writings of pilgrims, such as the female traveller Egeria, that there was a relic being exhibited as part of the True Cross in Jerusalem AD 380, just over half a century after Helena's reported discovery. Egeria also tells of a feast day that among other things celebrated the discovery of the True Cross.

The gospels clearly place Jesus's tomb and the site of his crucifixion outside the walls of Jerusalem, and yet visitors to Constantine's complex found the sepulchre and Mount Calvary set down in the very heart of the city. Evidence seems to suggest that alterations and extensions made to the Holy City, which helps to resolve this anomaly. Such expansion was partly due to Emperor Hadrian's rebuilding projects in the second century. Saewulf wrote that 'Emperor Hadrian . . . rebuilt the city and the Temple of the Lord and extended the city as far as the Tower of David, which formerly had been some distance from the city. Anyone can see from the Mount of Olives where the extreme west walls of the city formerly were and how much the city was afterwards extended.'[10]

Archaeologists have indeed discovered that a third city wall had been built in AD 41, eleven years after Christ's death. This wall now enclosed the site of the crucifixion within its boundary. It appears that in the first century the city walls were situated further in, making a far less expansive city than is seen today.

Apparently confirming the location of the original sepulchre in which Christ was lain to rest, an underground quarry was found beneath the fourth-century complex. According to Rufinus in AD 402, the three crosses were discovered in a quarry or well, which would seem to place their unearthing more conclusively to the site uncovered by Helena. It also seems possible that Jesus could have died thus on an outcrop of rock over such a pit. Inside the Holy Sepulchre today, one can identify the hollows cut away for the accommodation of rock tombs.

The Romans who captured Jerusalem in the first century AD had the capacity for great cruelty and savagery, the practice of crucifixion being one of their notoriously brutal means of punishment by death. The first-century Jewish historian Josephus provides a detailed account of the Roman methods of crucifixion. The discovery of a crucified skeleton in 1968, in a burial cave at Giv'at ha-Miutar, north-east of Jerusalem, offered further proof of the barbarism of its techniques. The skeleton, dated to the first century, shows that nails were passed through the ankle bones. His legs had also been deliberately fractured to hasten death through asphyxiation, a common Roman method. With the weight distributed between hands and feet, the process of death was a prolonged and agonising one that could last several hours or days.

Fortunately as emperor, Constantine was tolerant of and receptive to the growing power of Christianity in spite of his own pagan origins. Christianity was legalised in AD 313 and crucifixion later banned in AD 337. With time, Constantine came to adopt Christianity as his own faith and was baptised just before his death. Perhaps the most crucial event in Constantine's conversion occurred in AD 312, six years after he was pronounced emperor of Rome's western empire. In this year

Constantine set out to take Rome as the supreme leader of the empire and master of the city. One night he reported a vision of the cross which appeared over his encampment. The event touched Constantine profoundly and moved him to employ the symbol of the cross as the emblem on his men's shields. It became the talisman of Constantine and his army, and they went on to take Rome successfully on 28 October that year. The cross also became symbolic of spiritual victory and Christian triumph.

In the period between the fourth century and the Muslim Conquest of 638, Jerusalem was alive with pilgrimage activity. In the fifth century there was an inclination among many monks, including those from Egypt, to relocate to the Holy Land. With this new settlement came more records and topographical writings of the Holy Land. This in turn raised its profile and many more pilgrims arrived to witness it for themselves. Simultaneously, the formality of the pilgrims' visits increased as a more organised 'pilgrim circuit' was established. The sixth-century writings of Theodosius show this development most clearly.

> From the Tomb of the Lord it is fifteen paces to the place of Calvary. It is all under one roof. From the place of Calvary it is fifteen paces to Golgotha where the Lord's cross was discovered. From Golgotha it is two hundred paces to Holy Sion.[11]

On a meditative level, the devout pilgrim could now attempt to recreate the biblical events so familiar to him by retracing the footsteps of Christ. This was made tractable through organised tours for pilgrims from one location to another, with instruction on the events and sufferings of Christ in each. In modern times this idea has been taken further by the inhabitants of the town of San Pedro in the Phillippines. Here bloody recreations of the flagellation and crucifixion are an annual event.

> With him, therefore, I wish to ascend on to Mount Sion and behold what he did after this; but, first, I wish to be imprisoned with Peter, that with him I may be taught by Christ not to deny him but to pray.[12]

For Margery Kempe in the fifteenth-century this mental strategy greatly enhanced her experience on an emotional level:

> And this creature wept and sobbed as plenteously as though she had seen our Lord with her bodily eyes suffering his Passion at that time. Before her in her soul she saw him in truth by contemplation, and that caused her to have compassion.[13]

As early as the third century pilgrims had been travelling to the site on the River Jordan where it was believed Jesus had been baptised by John the Baptist. Here, they immersed themselves in its waters (Matt. 3: 16–17). Originally, baptisms had been offered by John the Baptist as a way of preparing the soul in anticipation of the Lord's coming. By imitation, pilgrims felt that they could prepare themselves in the same way.

> Too mile fro the Ded See
> In Jordan Pylgremys whasched be.[14]

The exact location of the holy baptism seems to have been passed down by word of mouth, but the fact that pilgrims were travelling to a specific site on the Jordan less than 200 years after Jesus' death is encouraging evidence. For many years at the end of the twentieth century, the Jordan valley was a dangerous area because of the Arab-Israeli conflict, but in 1984, when Israel and Jordan made peace, archaeologists were finally able to move in. Among the astounding discoveries they made were seven churches and a monastery which housed within it a large baptismal pool, most likely for pilgrims.

William Wey's medieval guide compiled in the fifteenth century advised the pilgrim on how best to prepare for a trip to the Jordan. Focusing his attentions on practical concerns. 'Also whan ye shall ryde to flume Jordan take wyth you out of Jerusalem brede, wyne, water, harde eggys and chese, and suche vytaylles as ye maye haue for two dayes. For by alle that waye there is none to selle.'[15]

The re-enactment of Jesus' baptism held special significance for the pilgrim. One of Jesus' grievances with the temple priests in Jerusalem was their rejection of the lame, sick, blind and deformed as unworthy and imperfect. Such citizens were also banned from entering the temple, according to the Mishnah, an ancient book of Jewish law. So Jesus began to offer his own baptisms to which all were welcome. Many of these took place at the Pool of Bethesda near the temple walls. Although Jewish doctrine was akin to the medieval belief that physical illness was an outward sign of moral weakness, their rules were far less lenient in their rejection of the 'impure' as unworthy of forgiveness. Many of the medieval pilgrims arriving in the Holy Land were the lame, blind and sick, all looking for mercy and a cure.

For the Holy Land, more so perhaps than for medieval Europe, this was a time when greater trust was placed in the power of faith healers than in the few available doctors. Equally, the gospels report over 100 instances of Jesus curing the sick or exorcising the possessed, and he drew great crowds and followers in the process.

While the first Muslim Conquest of 638 impeded progress as far as upkeep and maintenance of the sites was concerned, it did not deter the stalwart pilgrims from risking Muslim hostility by completing their journeys to the Holy Land. The face of Jerusalem also changed. Just as Jesus had warned, the majestic Jewish temple, once the power base of society, was pulled down in AD 70, forty years after his death. In its place, in the seventh century, the glistening Dome on the Rock was erected, which is still counted as one of Islam's most holy sites. Arab supremacy lasted until 870. With a short remission, the city of Jerusalem again fell to Arab governors until 969. The city and its pilgrims were also to endure the destruction of the Church of the Holy Sepulchre in 1009.

Against these odds, pilgrim numbers continued to increase throughout the eleventh century. With the first crusade in 1099, a Latin military presence in the Holy Land made for a more protected and comfortable milieu for the pilgrim. Meanwhile, the dangers of Muslim hostility were still ever present. The scars of their opposition were eradicated with the rebuilding of the Church of the Holy Sepulchre by the end of the twelfth century.

After the loss of Jerusalem to Saladin, the papacy attempted to control pilgrim traffic to the Holy Land. In 1215 Pope Innocent III imposed a four-year suspension on ships to the Holy Land while forces were mustered for a new crusade. A ban on financial and commercial dealings with the infidel were also set in place. In the fourteenth century pilgrims needed papal permission to go to the Holy Land. While

Greek Orthodox pilgrims worshipping at the Stone of Unction in the Church of the Holy Sepulchre. *John Crook*

in the power of the infidel, the Holy Land was considered excommunicate, and therefore any Latin pilgrim visiting it in the fourteenth century without the Pope's consent was likewise a spiritual outcast.

Prior to these rapidly turning tides of religious conflict, both Gregory of Nyssa and St Jerome, in the fourth century, were quick to point out that Jerusalem already had its own shortcomings as a city. They noted that in spite of the religious prestige lavished on Jerusalem, it was still a city like any other and subject to crime, prostitution, theft and murder.[16]

Equally, Saewulf speaks of the continuing risks prevalent even after the crusades. On the journey from the port of Jaffa to the city of Jerusalem, pilgrims came under attack from Saracens who hid themselves in the nooks and hollows of the mountains. These were sometimes Muslim Bedouin tribesmen, whose nomadic caravans dwelt in the wilderness surrounding the Holy City. For the weary pilgrims, it was those who fell behind their group through heat exhaustion, or those parties whose group was vulnerably small that fell prey. The enemy was swift and well practiced in his art. Familiar with the pilgrim practice of sewing money into their cloaks, they were assured of their winnings. Pilgrims would not be foolish enough as to leave their party to give companions a proper Christian burial. Their corpses were left to line the route as a reminder of the pilgrim's vulnerability in this foreign land.

In 1064 a German pilgrimage led by Gunther, Bishop of Bamberg, came under Muslim attack. This was the most severe pilgrim massacre recorded, and many of the party were plundered and killed. 'For shame! The Enemies of Christ leapt on the back of the priests of Christ and pursued them across the plains on horseback, urging their steeds on with spurs.'[17]

Even at sea concern was expressed for the safety of travelling pilgrims. Saewulf notes how on leaving Jerusalem he went by sea to Constantinople, hugging the coast all the way in fear of the Saracens if they crossed the open deep of the Adriatic. Pilgrims to the Holy Land were also subject to another of the Saracen's practices, that of exacting charges, bargains and gifts. Pilgrims still found themselves paying protection dues, known as 'khafara', along the roads.

From the fourteenth century, a Franciscan community, based on Mount Sion, also worked for the interest and safety of the Latin pilgrim. Nothing, though, could shield the pilgrim from the different customs, mannerisms and mentalities that they would encounter in the Saracens. Brother Felix Faber went so far as to write a guide for pilgrims that would go some way to preparing them. His advice is particular, but prudent: for example, pilgrims should not make a show of laughter or merriment in front of the Saracens, lest the Saracens become suspicious of this and think the pilgrims are laughing at them. Pilgrims should also be careful not to stare at their women. Equally important, pilgrims should not offend the Saracens by wearing white turbans, or winding white cloths about their heads, as this was not their privilege. Other restrictions that Latin pilgrims did well to remember were that they were forbidden entry into the mosques or into cities other than on foot. Faber also noted that the Saracens were easily vexed by pilgrims who stepped over the tombs of their dead.

The tide of religious conquest was to turn again when in the thirteenth century the Holy Land was lost to the Muslims once more. This time the damage to the pilgrim industry was irreparable. Rome became favoured over Jerusalem as a far less risky undertaking. The Holy Land's popularity as the cradle of sacred history was undercut by the very nature of religious fervour itself.

In the periods during which the Holy Land was under Muslim control, it was in the best interests of Christian pilgrims arriving in Arab-occupied territory to follow safe procedure. This involved securing the correct paperwork in order to be granted access. Sir John Mandeville notes that the Sultan gave his signet, or seal, as approval of entry, which the pilgrims carried before them for the duration of their visit. Mandeville, who visited Jerusalem more as tourist than as pilgrim, has us believe that he was the subject of special treatment. His admittance to the temple by the Church of the Holy Sepulchre was secured with letters carrying the seal of the Sultan: 'he strictly commanded his subjects to let me see all the places I wanted, and to show me the relics and the holy places as I wished.'[18]

Margery Kempe, as a lone female pilgrim, also portrays her Saracen guides as courteous and accommodating. 'The Saracens also made much of her, and conveyed and escorted her about the country wherever she wanted to go.'[19]

Not all, though, were as impressed by their hosts. Felix Faber's first visit to the Holy Land in 1480 is recorded as a bit of a disappointment. His stay there lasted only nine days in all as a result of the hurried, rather perfunctory tours offered by the Saracen guides. This is reflective of the ephemeral, formal nature of the tours that were being offered to accommodate an ever increasing number of pilgrims. Faber on the other hand was keen to rest, reflect and meditate on the sites he had witnessed.

He relates that as well as being rushed through the sites, he was not permitted to visit all of them, he could not walk over the Mount of Olives more than once as he had desired and was taken to Bethlehem and Bethany in the dark!

There is evidence to suggest that other measures were taken by the Arabs to manage their new-found enterprise, for example at individual sites where a limited number of pilgrims were allowed in at a time. The Holy Sepulchre, as the most popular venue, was one such example. Theoderich describes its six doors, each guarded by a strict porter who allowed no fewer than six or more than twelve to enter at a time. Faber states that it was no more than two at a time on his visit. He also highlights the irony of the circumstances of his visit:

> We went by them with shame and blushing because it is a great confusion that Christ's faithful worshippers should be let in by Christ's blasphemers.[20]

Heightening the intensity of his experience was the convergence of western and eastern Christians within such sites, each with their own practices of worship. Faber becomes mildly irritated by the disorderly clamouring and outcries of his eastern compatriots, blaming them also for the extraordinary number of fleas!

Clearly, such pilgrim groups had quickly come to represent a profitable industry, and it was in the interests of the Muslim authorities to see as many pass through their gates as possible. Such large groups and the popularity of the sites brought some drawbacks. Mandeville describes the conservation action that the Muslim authorities were forced to take within the Holy Sepulchre:

> Because some men who went there used to try to break bits of the stone off to take away with them, the Sultan had a wall built round the Tomb so that nobody could touch it except on the left side.[21]

Brother Faber also describes how one pilgrim removed a piece from the Monastery of St Catherine on Mount Sinai and warned that removal of rock from the Holy Sepulchre was punishable by excommunication. We are also reminded of the diversity of social class among the pilgrims in the regulations laid out regarding defacement of the Sepulchre's walls. It seems that those of noble birth were in the habit of marking the walls of holy sites with their coat of arms or else attaching images of their arms to ensure they had marked their being there for all to see. Some graffiti can still be seen on the walls of the sepulchre complex, such as the intriguing drawing of a medieval galley. Underneath are the words, *Domine Ivimus*, or Master, we have arrived. This grafitti and its accompanying words palpably exude the grateful relief of having survived hell and high water to arrive at their destination.

The rock walls also served another purpose, its crannies playing host to numerous bundles of hair. For those wishing for a cure from toothache, beards were shaven

A graffito of a medieval galley, with the words *Domine Ivimus*, Master, we have arrived, found during excavations behind the Armenian Chapel of St Helena in the Church of the Holy Sepulchre. It appears to be evidence for a very early pilgrimage to Jerusalem. *John Crook*

and left there in hope of divine dispensation of a cure. For those seeking relief from headaches, the head was shaved and the hair left to the sepulchre's guardians to be placed on the spot where the True Cross was found.

Having visited the Holy Sepulchre, pilgrims could follow the Via Dolorosa, the route that Christ had taken bearing the cross on his back, as well as climb Mount Sion where Christ washed his disciples' feet and where stood a chapel marking the holy places of the Last Supper. Mount Sion had also been witness to much other historical biblical activity that assured it of pilgrim interest. For example, it was here that St Peter wept over Christ's Passion. Most importantly though, the Last Supper had seen the gathering here of Christ and his disciples in the guest-room of a well-to-do house. It was on this occasion that Jesus announced that one of them would betray him.

Afterwards, Jesus and his disciples had made their way back to Bethany, a town of much less volatile political climate than Jerusalem and safer for Jesus. Another popular pilgrim stop, it hosted the site of Lazarus' resurrection and tomb, and the house of his sister, Martha. Stopping on their climb up the Mount of Olives, Jesus had rested in the Garden of Gethsemane, still marked out by olive trees today as it was 2,000 years ago. This site was and is highly charged with significance for the pilgrim. It is here that Jesus experienced his agony, when he became resigned to the certainty of his impending suffering and death. The emotional depth of his

A modern view of Jerusalem looking towards the Holy Sepulchre. *John Crook*

suffering and grief at this prospect is one that has attracted pilgrim interest on a very profound and human level. Just before dawn the Roman soldiers arrived, accompanied by the man whose name has come to evoke the very epitome of treachery and betrayal, Judas.

Among the other reported pilgrim attractions were the stone that had sealed the mouth of the tomb, a piece of the pillar to which Christ was bound when scourged, the burial place of St Stephen and the sites of the Doubting Thomas scene and Christ's first reappearance to his disciples after the resurrection. Pilgrims also climbed to the summit of the mountain just above Jericho on which Christ had fasted for forty days and nights while enduring Satan's temptations of power and material wealth. This was sometimes referred to as 'Mount Quarantine' which originally meant a duration of forty days. Medieval accounts tell us of the challenge that this journey imposed on visiting pilgrims. One account described it as 'passyngly hote and ryght hyghe.'[22]

Margery Kempe also described how her own struggle was resolved:

And there she asked her companion to help her up the mountain, and they said 'no' as they could barely help themselves up. . . . And just then, a Saracen, a good-looking man, happened to come by her . . . took her under his arm and led her up the high mountain.[23]

William Wey's fifteenth-century guide also offered practical advice on descending the mountain:

> And when ye come downe agayne for any thynge drynke noo water, but reste you a lytyll. And thenne ete brede and drynke clere wyne wythout water, for water after that grete heete gendreth a flyxe or a fuour, or both that many one have deyed therof.[24]

The stalwart pilgrim could go on to visit many of the other significant holy sites, such as the birthplace of John the Baptist occupied by the Chapel of the Franciscan Monastery of St John, Cana, or the Church of the Tomb of the Virgin in the Valley of Kedron. Another ass ride took the pilgrim to Bethlehem to the Church of the Basilica of the Nativity, beneath which were two grottoes attributed to the site of the holy manger and Christ's birth. Another three days' journey from Bethlehem was rewarded with the arrival at the birthplace of the Virgin Mary at Nazareth. It seems that it was customary also to return to the Holy Sepulchre to make a second visit,

The star marks the traditional site of Christ's nativity in the Church of the Basilica of the Nativity, Bethlehem. *John Crook*

perhaps to the Chapel of the Apparition where Christ had appeared to his mother on the morning of his resurrection.

With its demanding but unique itinerary the pilgrim's journey to the Holy Land offered a host of different experiences, emotions and challenges that were unrivalled by many other pilgrimage sites, and, for a time, unsurpassed in popularity.

CHAPTER THREE

ROME

I strongly recommend the wonderful panorama of the whole city. There is so great a forest of towers and so many palatial buildings, that no one has counted them.[1]

A safer and less costly destination than the Holy Land awaited the pilgrim in Western Europe at the seat of the Roman Catholic Church. When travel to the East was ill advised, Rome comfortably replaced Jerusalem in the popularity stakes. Equally, it had always ranked as a notable and accessible stop en route to Jerusalem.

> After these things had happened, Paul made up his mind to travel through Macedonia and Achaia and go on to Jerusalem. 'After I go there,' he said, 'I must also see Rome.'[2]

There were few Christological objects referred to in the Bible that had not been claimed to survive as holy artefacts. In Rome the most significant of these were the bones of the chief apostles, Peter and Paul, those relics of martyrs killed during the persecutions of the Emperor Diocletian and many more fantastic vestiges, including phials of Christ's blood, the Virgin's milk and even Jesus's footprint![3]

The pilgrimage Church of Santa Croce today claims ownership of the *titulus crucis*, and eminent scholars, such as Carsten Peter Thiede, have worked towards proving its authenticity.[4] Modern visitors to Santa Croce can also ponder the purported fragment of the good thief's cross. Perhaps most debatable is Santa Croce's apparently preserved finger of Doubting Thomas.

In the mid-fourth century a Roman liturgical calendar listed around thirty sanctuaries of saints in and around Rome. Equally important were the plentiful opportunities for pilgrims to receive indulgence. Margery Kempe's account speaks of a man who recently converted to Christianity: he 'went on many pilgrimages to Rome and to many other places to gain pardon'.[5] Charlemagne also visited Rome on four separate occasions in order to perform his religious duties at the holy sites. It was while in Rome in AD 800 that the Pope crowned him as head of the Holy Roman Empire.

John Capgrave, prior of King's Lynn, theologian and chronicler, made a pilgrimage to Rome in *c.* 1450 from which his *Ye Solace of Pilgrimes* was written. Among the profusion of information he contributes on the notable sites of Rome, he offers a description of the head relics of SS Peter and Paul in the Church of St John in the Lateran. These are exhibited to the public, he tells us, the week before Easter, Peter's with its full grey beard and Paul's with its long face and red beard.[6]

Rome offered the pilgrim something very different. First, its law had forbidden the burial of its dead within the city walls. Most pilgrims would have been accustomed to visiting a holy shrine within the hallowed precinct of a cathedral, church or other religious complex. In order to see the burial sites of Rome's early martyrs the pilgrim was required to follow the roadsides outside Rome. Psychologically, this must have been a very different experience for the pilgrim. Medieval religious belief meant that the spiritual puissance of a holy figure was localised within the confines of a holy place such as a church or cathedral. Also, the shrine was usually situated in a place that held a strong association with the life or death of the holy figure. The discovery of rows of buried martyrs along the roadside outside the city walls of Rome introduced an alternative experience for pilgrims not used to venerating a holy figure in this way.

Secondly, Rome had many spectacular buildings from its pre-Christian days. Sites such as the Colosseum awoke a more aesthetic and historical interest within many pilgrims, as some of their accounts show. Master Gregorius in his *Narracio de Mirabilibus Urbis Romae* (or *Marvels of Rome*), written in the late twelfth or early

The Colosseum, Rome. *Sarah Hopper*

thirteenth century, is one such example. The author's preoccupation and fascination with the classical sites of the city is clearly apparent, so that the important patriarchal basilica of St Peter's is mentioned only in passing. Of the Colosseum he states that there are not the words to justify its magnificence and splendour.

Gregorius also offers an interesting insight into the working of the medieval mind. Surrounded by these wondrous vestiges of Classical Rome, pilgrims attached stories of Christian significance to some of them, perhaps to endorse them as religious attractions and justify their profane curiosity. Dismissive of these Christian associations, Gregorius declares that he will spare his readers the 'worthless stories of pilgrims'.[7] Of another site embellished by pilgrims in this way he says, 'It's an utterly worthless tale, typical of those told by pilgrims.'[8]

An example was the obelisk described by Gregorius in St Peter's Square. At its summit was a bronze sphere believed to contain the ashes of Julius Caesar, as it marked the site where he had been warned of the conspiracy for his assassination. Pilgrims affectionately addressed the obelisk as St Peter's Needle, associating it with the site of the apostle's martyrdom. Master Gregorius describes how pilgrims attempted to crawl into the space between the obelisk and its base (it was supported on four feet). In so doing, the pilgrim understood that he was performing true penance, and thus would receive remission of his sins. This was commonly practiced by pilgrims at the shrines of Edward the Confessor and St Thomas at Canterbury, for example, where they reached, even climbed through the niches of the shrine. Not only does Gregorius's account highlight the need within the medieval pilgrim for spiritual atonement, but also the necessity for a tangible, visible object in order for this to be fulfilled. In this instance, pilgrims to Rome had essentially created an object of veneration out of a pagan, classical monument.

After much persecution and subjugation, Christianity was eventually established as the accepted religion in Rome in AD 313. This event was pioneered by Emperor Constantine from AD 306–37. Constantine was also partly responsible for the building of basilicas to house the sites of holy significance, most importantly the graves of SS Peter and Paul. Apocryphal accounts to the New Testament note that Peter had gone to Rome as the spearhead of a project to spread the gospel, his status endorsed by his close association with Christ as friend and follower.

After Christ's death, in the mid-first century, Rome grew into a thriving centre for Christianity, for which the Emperor Nero had little tolerance. In AD 64, eleven of Rome's fourteen districts were ravaged by a great fire. In the ensuing blame and punishment that Nero apportioned to the Christians of Rome, it is believed by many that Peter and Paul both perished. Tradition holds that Peter had requested an inverted crucifixion, as he felt unworthy of dying in the same way as Christ. As a Roman citizen, Paul was granted a more noble execution – decapitation.

In the volatile, political climate of the greater part of the Middle Ages Rome had its fair share of invasion and attack. In 568, after the final decline of the Roman Empire in the fifth century, Rome was invaded by the Lombards, a Germanic people from the north, originally known as Longobardi on account of the long spears they carried. This left Rome struggling with disease and food shortages as well as structural damage to its buildings, aqueducts and monuments. It was after another siege by the Lombards in 756, that the decision was taken to rebury Rome's martyrs within the city walls for their preservation.

The Crucifixion of St Peter, Michelangelo Buonarotti (1475–1564). *Cappella Paolina, Vatican/Bridgeman Art Library*

The upkeep and repair of damaged catacombs and classical buildings depended on the available economic resources as well as the occupant of the papal seat at the time. Some Popes took greater care in the maintenance of the city's heritage than others. For example, Pope Innocent III (1198–1216) was less concerned with the upkeep of the city's ecclesiastical buildings than with the construction of a new and fortified papal mansion on the site of the present Vatican. Evidence suggests that

cabis me in equitate tua.
Educes de tribulacione animam meam et in misericordia tua disperdes omnes inimicos meos.
Et perdes omnes qui tribulant animam meam quoniam ego seruus tuus sum.
Gloria patri et filio et spiritu sancto.
Sicut erat in principio et nunc et semper et in secula seculorum. Amen.
Et remniscans Ant. domine delicta nostra vel parentum nostrorum neque uindictam sumas de preccatis nostris parce domine populo tuo quem redemisti sanguine tuo proprio ne in eternum irascaris nobis. Lect.

Rome's monuments and catacombs went through periods of such disrepair at times that pilgrim numbers decreased.

Nonetheless, in the midst of such turmoil, stalwart and resolute pilgrims continued journeying to Rome to bear witness to its host of important basilicas and venerated sites. Inevitably though, during such post-siege periods, pilgrims who relied heavily on the sustenance and shelter available along their path found themselves struggling as a result of the city's overly stretched resources. In the sixth century, for example, Pope Gregory the Great resolved to assist the impoverished and needy among the increasing number of pilgrims in the city. Gregory also sent papal missions into the rest of Europe, attracting pilgrims from France, Spain and Germany, and with them the custom which would help restart the city's idling financial engine. This increased surge of pilgrims from Europe coincided with Christian refugees escaping the Muslim–Arab oppression in Syria, Palestine and Egypt, who arrived in the Mediterranean. While Rome's resources and facilities were still being stretched, its profile as a religious centre with an incisive role to play was being inexorably raised. While addressing poverty in Rome, Gregory chose not to use the money allocated for the building of new ecclesiastical buildings. He was shrewd enough, however, to order the construction of an annular crypt in St Peter's that preserved the precious relics, while facilitating the easy flow of pilgrims and their offerings.

A historic proclamation by Pope Boniface VIII in 1300 marked Rome's most significant turn of events as a pilgrimage destination. This year was to mark the first of Rome's jubilee years, which brought pilgrims flooding through its gates. Originally a feature of the Jewish calendar, the jubilee symbolised a year of absolution and atonement for all sins committed. Boniface offered plenary indulgence to all those pilgrims visiting the Basilica of St Peter and the other saints of Rome within this year.

In the thirteenth century, Rome's population stood at around 35,000.[9] With the marking of the first jubilee year at the end of the thirteenth century, numbers were set to rise due to increasing pilgrim numbers on top of the resident population.[10] In the jubilee year of 1450 plenary remission was made available to all those penitents who stayed in Rome for at least fifteen days and made a daily visit to the four patriarchal basilicas of Rome.[11]

In the jubilee year of 2000, a staggering 20–30 million Roman Catholic pilgrims were expected, on top of the large numbers of tourists that visit the city each year. Today Rome still struggles with the repercussions of being such an important religious centre. In contrast to the notion of pious duty that the Medieval Church promoted, modern pilgrims are requested to keep the length of their stay to a minimum in order reduce the strain on resources. Pilgrims are also encouraged to seek their accommodation outside the capital.

The practical reasons for this have been highlighted in Rome's history as a pilgrimage centre. In the jubilee of 1450 172 pilgrims perished among stampeding crowds, others died when the Ponte d'Angelo collapsed under sheer weight of pilgrims in the jubilee of 1300 and many others starved as a result of the city's exhausted food supply. Rome was by no means the only popular pilgrimage centre

Opposite: The procession of Pope Gregory the Great to end the plague in Rome. *Très Heures du Duc de Berry* (early fifteenth century). *Musée Condé, Chantilly, France/Bridgeman Art Library*

to suffer such disasters; at Vézelay in 1120 a fire is said to have killed 1,000 pilgrims.

Needless to say, the piety and devotion required of modern-day pilgrims is no less regarded. In fact, a Papal Bull issued at the end of 1998 suggests that today plenary indulgence is offered under much stricter terms than during the medieval jubilees. Aside from going to confession, communion and visiting the holy sites of Rome and the Holy Land, the penitent is required to offer his or her services in charitable work, such as visiting the incarcerated and the sick, attending to the elderly and undertaking voluntary work.

A large sign notifies the modern jubilee pilgrims of their duties in Rome's churches before they enter:

Sacramental confession (made within 20 days) and Holy Communion.
Participation in Holy Mass or another liturgical celebration or devotion
(for example, the Rosary or Stations of the Cross).
Eucharist worship or meditation and recitation of Our Father, the Creed,
a Marian Prayer (Ave Maria, Salve Regina).

Initially, in 1300, the jubilee had been due to take place every centenary, but its celebration was then increased to every fifty years, thus improving the chances of

Basilica of St Peter and the Vatican. *John Crook*

every man and woman being able to benefit from it in their lifetimes. In 1470, it was increased to every quarter century. Rome's financial resources also stood to benefit from pilgrimage custom in the offerings made to its churches. An account of the jubilee of 1300 directly states that the offerings made by pilgrims accrued great wealth for the Church and the Roman people so that 'all were made rich by their takings.'[12] In the popular jubilee of 1450 Pope Nicholas V deposited healthy sums into the Medici bank.

There were other similar celebrations of forgiveness and atonement in the Christian calendar that originated outside of Rome. In her dictated account, Margery Kempe describes how she arrived at the Portiuncula chapel (where St Francis had worshipped) in Assisi on Lammas Day. This was marked on 1 August as a day of indulgence, originally granted to St Francis by Pope Honorius III. Kempe underlines the day's significance as one of: 'great pardon with plenary remission, in order to obtain grace, mercy and forgiveness for herself, for all her friends, for all her enemies, and for all the souls in purgatory.'[13]

A fifteenth-century account gives the pilgrim circuits of full indulgence as comprising seven churches, although the pilgrim churches of Rome numbered many more.[14] Those of indulgence are included below, the first four constituting Rome's patriarchal basilicas. All continue to be of unique interest to the modern pilgrim.

BASILICA OF ST PETER

The majestic Basilica of St Peter is built around a tomb wherein tradition holds Peter's body was placed after his martyrdom. The Circo Vaticano of Nero's reign once stood in the area of the present basilica, and it seems that many Christians met their untimely end here between AD 64 and 67. There are indeed remains of a first-century tomb beneath the foundations of the church, but nothing to conclude it is that of St Peter. The basilica marked the hub of Christianity in Rome, and nearby were monasteries, taverns, shops, hostels and all manner of vendors and money changers to service the pilgrim.

BASILICA DI SANTA MARIA MAGGIORE

This building has an intriguing legend attached to its construction. Similar to the conception of Walsingham in Norfolk, the Basilica of Santa Maria Maggiore began in 352 with a vision. Legend has it that the Virgin Mary appeared to Pope Liberius instructing him to build a church on the spot where snow had fallen. The next day (at the beginning of August), snow had miraculously covered the summit of the Esquiline Hill in Rome, and so it was there that construction began.

Inside the baldacchino covers a porphyry sarcophagus holding the relics of many martyrs, including St Matthew.

Overleaf: The interior of the Basilica of St Peter. *John Crook*

Page 38: Basilica di San Paulo Fuori le Mura. *Sarah Hopper*

BASILICA DI SAN GIOVANNI IN LATERANO

Founded by Constantine in the fourth century, this basilica is important as the Pope's seat as Bishop of Rome. The Gothic baldacchino over the papal altar is said to contain many relics, most notably the heads of SS Peter and Paul. Of note also are the transept frescoes that depict the conversion of Constantine to Christianity.

BASILICA DI SAN PAULO FUORI LE MURA

St Paul's head is said to rest in the Basilica di San Giovanni in Laterano; the rest of his remains are in the Basilica of St Paul outside the walls of Rome. The original church was built by Constantine the Great in the fourth century over Paul's burial site. Until the construction of St Peter's, San Paolo was held to be the largest church in the world. Today's building is a modern construction built after a fire in 1823 that destroyed the former church.

CHURCH OF SANTA CROCE IN GERUSALEMME

Thought to have been founded in AD 320 by Constantine's mother, Empress Helena, this church was thus endowed with some of the most prized holy relics. Believed to be among these were a piece of the True Cross brought by Helena from Jerusalem to Rome. The fifteenth-century apse frescoes expound the legend of the True Cross. At the rear exterior of the church the remains of Helena's imperial palace are still visible.

BASILICA DI SAN LORENZO FUORI LE MURA

St Lawrence was burnt at the stake under Roman Emperor Valerian in AD 258. His life and marytrdom are expounded in the preserved portico frescoes. Erected under Constantine in the fourth century, it was rebuilt in the sixth century and saw many further alterations between the eighth and thirteenth centuries. The remains of SS Stephen and Lawrence are kept beneath the high altar in the church's crypt.

BASILICA DI SAN SEBASTIANO

Built in AD 340, this basilica is prestigiously located over some of the catacombs of Rome wherein the bodies of SS Peter and Paul were harboured during the Christian repression and persecution under Vespasian (AD 69–79). For this reason, it was originally known as the *Memoria Apostolorum,* or Memory (or Remembrance) of the Apostles. The nave we see today was constructed in 1612 and has a small reliquary chapel leading off it. Within it is an arrow that is believed to be one which was used to kill St Sebastian, martyred in the late third century, as well as a piece of the column to which he was tied when he was scourged. The altar of St Sebastian in the basilica is located directly over the burial place of the saint in the catacombs beneath.

Also of interest are the catacombs of Rome, those of St Sebastian holding the greatest significance. During the Christian persecutions, the bodies of SS Peter and

Paul were brought to the catacombs for safety. While from the fourth century pilgrims could visit the basilicas of SS Peter and Paul to venerate their remains, the location of the catacombs was still venerated as the hiding place of Christians in perilous times.

Dug by hand, seven miles of tunnels stretch through the tufa rock in each direction. Arranged on three levels, the walls hold the remains of about 160,000 people, neatly tucked into niches and arches. A visit to the catacombs today inspires a sense of wonder at the eery stillness and seemingly infinite expanse of their passages. The temperature maintains itself at a cool fifteen degrees celsius, and its tunnels take you eighteen metres below ground, at their deepest point. The names 'Pietre et Paule' are written repeatedly on the walls, about 604 times, in one area of the catacombs by way of prayers and invocations scored into the tufa. This is probably the place where their bodies were laid.

For the modern pilgrim, the catacombs of St Sebastian are very interesting. At one point, the tunnels open out onto the remains of an ancient Roman crematorium. Pottery urns holding the ashes of the dead are surrounded by pagan imagery and decoration of the type that the Roman Catholic Church had worked so

Pilgrims touching the foot of the statue of St Peter in the Basilica of St Peter. *John Crook*

hard to obliterate. Dating from about AD 130, the site of this Roman crematorium was reused by Constantine the Great. Between AD 340 and 1919 they remained undetected and unknown by the pilgrims that visited there.

The chronicler Adam of Usk made his way to Rome in 1402 and was quickly appointed papal chaplain in the apostolic chapel. He was in lodgings near St Peter's for four years. His descriptions of Rome offer us a first-hand account of the city in the fifteenth century, and an insight into its vices. He voices concerns that Rome had become a hotbed of financial intrigue and competitive investment. Such vices also threatened the priesthood who were taking bribes.

> everything was for sale, and benefices were granted not according to merit but to the highest bidder; where anyone with more money than sense who sought to rise in the world would bank his money with merchants . . . to secure his promotion.[15]

Many guidebooks were produced to cater for the large number of pilgrims travelling to Rome. They served pilgrims as a manual offering assistance in all aspects of travel and safety. They existed as early as the third century, volunteering advice on sites worthy of visit, either in Rome or en route Santiago de Compostela in Spain.

While earlier guides tended to focus more on the novelty of Rome's classical buildings and history, later offerings adopted a more itineraric approach listing burial places and Christian shrines worthy of visit. By the fifteenth century, many were also offering advice on how much each of the sites was worth in indulgences, such as the guide written by the Augustinian friar John Capgrave. Other accounts, such as Brewyn's *A Fifteenth-Century Guide Book to the Principal Churches of Rome*, included invaluable advice on journey distances and rates of exchange. An earlier thirteenth-century guide, the *Mirabilia Urbis Romae*, chose to focus on the early Christian legends and stories attached to the city. Such manuals must also have served as an 'armchair guide' for those unable to undertake pilgrimage.

Rome was popular as a destination for pilgrims as its many churches readily facilitated the pilgrim's pious motives for indulgence and atonement while also offering a tantalising glimpse into its pagan past, and it was easier for Latin pilgrims to get to than the Holy Land. The papacy's shrewd and systematic organisation of indulgences within Rome equally assured its prevalence on the pilgrim itinerary.

Opposite: Trajan's Column, Rome. *Sarah Hopper*

CHAPTER FOUR

SANTIAGO DE COMPOSTELA

The site became known as Compostela – the star field – and there a city had arisen that drew travellers from every part of the Christian world. These travellers were called pilgrims, and their symbol was the scallop shell.[1]

From the tenth century, Santiago de Compostela, in the Galician region of Spain, became an increasingly popular choice with pilgrims. Its patron saint is James, who, according to tradition, was murdered on the orders of King Herod in AD 44, while returning home to Jerusalem from Spain. His journey to Spain had been a religious mission to convert the country's people to Christianity. Rescued from the Atlantic surf, St James's body commanded reverence as a highly important Christian martyr.

As an apostle of Christ, St James's shrine naturally came to rank highly among those of his European counterparts. Equally enticing was the legend surrounding the story of his corpse's rescue and its transportation to a burial site. Friends of the saint were said to have placed it in a boat sailing through the Mediterranean, the Straits of Gibraltar and along the Iberian coast, landing at the town of Iria Flavia, today known as Padrón. Having disembarked the body, it was laid on a rock, which miraculously metamorphosed into a stone coffin enclosing the corpse. Variations on the theme relate how the pagan Queen Lupa was persuaded to permit burial of the body in her land, whereupon she sent the men into the hills. Significantly, it is recorded that she was converted to Christianity as a result of the prestigious arrival and burial.

From this point, it seems that the corpse and its miraculous recovery faded from memory until its rediscovery in the ninth century. It was unearthed by an unassuming shepherd named Pelayo, who, legend states, was led to the spot where the apostle lay by a star. Following this, popular etymology created the name 'Compostela' from *Campus Stellae* or 'field of the star'. It seems more probable, though, that the name was derived from the Latin for burial ground, *compostum*, as archaeological work has uncovered other burials in the surrounding area. Nevertheless, such a theory created further romantic association with the saint

Opposite: A statue of St James the Great as a pilgrim in the doorway of the cathedral at Santiago de Compostela. *Mary Evans Picture Library*

and the legend of his burial forged an enduring tradition in the history of medieval pilgrimage.

The earliest chronicled pilgrim to Compostela was the Bishop of Puy from France in AD 951. Today, thousands of pilgrims make the rigorous journey to its princely cathedral to pay homage to Christ's apostle. Many of these are students, aged between twenty-six and thirty, but many more pensioners and professionals also take part in the popular months of July and August. The recent Holy Year of 1999 saw pilgrim numbers in excess of 150,000.

In 1121, the far-reaching influence of the cult of St James saw Henry I found an abbey in Reading, England. It was endorsed as another esteemed centre of the cult by its hallowed relic, the hand of the saint, said to have been brought back from Spain by the daughter of Henry, Empress Matilda. Its veneration by visiting pilgrims assured the abbey's glory and eminence until the Dissolution.

Spain's political history saw periods of instability and upheaval over the years at the hands of the Romans, Visigoths, the Islamic Moors and Christians in their

Charlemagne and his army fighting the Saracens in Spain in 778, from the story of Ogier, Antoine Verard (fifteenth century). *Private Collection/Bridgeman Art Library*

resolute crusades to the area. In 711 the Moors had arrived from northern Africa and succeeded in infiltrating almost every part of Spain. The burial of the Christian apostle coincided with this Islamic invasion and the ensuing efforts of Spanish Christians toward self-preservation. In spite of this upheaval, it was at this time that Spain experienced a significant advance in pilgrimage activity, a period of strengthened unity and resolve in the name of Christianity.

Simultaneously, the capacity of Spain's patron saint was augmented with his newly attributed roles of warrior and protector. The reason behind Spain's decision to actively counter the Arab invasion came, as so often in medieval tradition, with a dream. Charlemagne reported a dream in which St James had appeared, imploring him to free the land of his burial from Arab domination. His own involvement in the battle against the Moors was fuelled by the inspiration he took from his dream. Just as Homer had recorded the intervention of immortal gods in the wars waged by man, legends began to speak of the figure of St James entering the battle at Clavajo in 859 on a white charger and named *Santiago Matamoros*, or 'St James the Moorslayer'. The tympana of Galicia's churches are often shown with images of the saint in this proactive, belligerent guise. St James had become more than just a venerated figure of saintly virtue, he was active and crucial in rescuing Christianity in Spain.

For the pilgrim, the journey to Spain assumed greater impetus in the light of Christianity's struggle there. It was perhaps felt among pilgrims that they were assisting the cause through their presence and spiritual practice there. For others, their pilgrimage became a crusade in which they became active in the conflict. It is perhaps no surprise, therefore, that the reclaiming of Spain coincided with the peak of Compostela's popularity with pilgrims.

Compostela became firmly marked on the map in the year 1100 when it received Diego Gelmirez as its first archbishop in nearly fifteen years. In 1120, Compostela was named as a metropolitan see by Pope Callixtus II and Gelmirez' post was elevated to that of archbishop. Although not all of Gelmirez' actions and beliefs were supported by the people of Compostela, the naming of an archbishop had endorsed the city's recognition as a key religious centre.

Originally known as the *Codex Callixtenus*, as its authorship was wrongly attributed to Pope Callixtus II, the *Liber Sancti Jacobi* was a guidebook that served to further promote the cult of St James and encourage pilgrims to make the journey to Compostela. Dating from the mid-twelfth century, the assembly of its five books was credited to a French cleric named Aimery Picaud of Parthenay Le Vieux. It laid down the correct modes of behaviour and devotion for pilgrims, as well as offering advice and warning on all other aspects of pilgrimage, such as routes and hostels.

The first book contained a series of songs and hymns, the second expounded twenty-two miracles attributed to St James (mostly through his intervention in the religious wars). The third book offered an anthology of stories relating to the life of St James and the legends surrounding the discovery of his tomb, while the fourth covered the history of Charlemagne's campaigns against the Moors in the eighth century. The fifth and final book was the pilgrim's guide, and outlined the main pilgrim's routes though France and Spain that led to Compostela, as well as pointing out the chief shrines along the way. Its pages also presented some candidly expressed opinions on the different peoples that the pilgrim would encounter on his journey. The Basques were described as a wicked and untrustworthy people, who were savage, perfidious and ugly![2]

A signpost on the Via Podiensis to Santiago de Compostela. *John Crook*

Santiago de Compostela was also to influence pilgrimage in another way. The scallop shell of St James became such a well recognised pilgrim token as to become the symbol of medieval pilgrimage as a whole. This was frequently echoed in contemporary art and literature. Formerly worn to denote the completion of a journey to the shrine of St James, the scallop came to be worn by any man or woman who had made pilgrimage to any venerated site in his native country or beyond. Equally, St James's many roles as patron saint of Spain, holy apostle, warrior protector and miracle-performing martyr were increased to include patron saint of all pilgrims. He began to be depicted in pilgrim's garb and wearing the scallop shell in his hat.

Over 200 shells have been discovered in pilgrim burials dating from the ninth to the seventeenth century, from 160 sites around Europe.[3] Even at the time the archbishops of Compostela attempted to limit the sale of scallop shell tokens in an effort to retain the emblem's exclusive association with the city. Such widespread adoption of the scallop shell by pilgrims makes it difficult to definitively prove the popularity of Compostela.

As with most principal pilgrim routes, those that led to Compostela through France and Spain were punctuated by inns, hospitals, monastic provision and chapels to ensure the pilgrim's physical and spiritual preservation. In the eleventh century St Domingo de la Calzada was one who devoted his work to the founding of further pilgrim's hostels and the improvement of pilgrim routes. When the popularity of pilgrimage to Compostela was at its height, it was estimated that hostels were sufficiently located within a day's walk of each other. Modern pilgrims can still benefit from the provision of refugios along the way, including many in the mountains and in the environs of Compostela. Today these are still run by religious orders, as well as individuals and sympathetic councils who provide basic accommodation and rely purely upon pilgrim donations of roughly £3 per night. Popular and well established is the Refugio El Gaucelmo at Rabanal, rebuilt by the Confraternity of St James in London.

Awaiting the weary pilgrim at the end of his journey was the Cathedral of Santiago de Compostela. Built in the eleventh century, it conformed to the model of French basilicas such as those of Ste Foy at Conques, St Sernin at Toulouse and St Martin at Tours, all of which could be visited by the overland pilgrim depending on the route taken. Having conquered the hill of Monte del Gozo outside the city, from which point the cathedral and its bell tower were a welcome sight, the majority of pilgrims would then have entered the city through the north-east gate. The Porta Francigena, or French Gate, as the majority of pilgrims came through France.

The Via Francigena, a road lined with hospitals and street traders, would lead the pilgrim to an open square on the cathedral's north side, referred to as 'Paradise'. It is richly described in chapter nine of the *Liber Sancti Jacobi*'s fifth book as the place

A pilgrim travelling to Santiago de Compostela on the Via Podiensis in France. *John Crook*

The west front of the Cathedral of St James, Santiago de Compostela. *John Crook*

where pilgrims could purchase their scallop shells as well as other essentials such as medicines, purses, shoes and belts.[4]

Entrance to the cathedral would have been through the majestic yet graceful Portico de la Gloria, carved between 1168 and 1188 by Master Mateo. Its Romanesque stonework is richly adorned with apostles, the transfiguration of Christ and the welcoming figure of a seated St James over the central column. No doubt the pilgrim would have stopped to ponder the chorus of prophets and apostles, a welcoming assembly which flanked the great doorway. Happily, this spectacle is still available to the modern pilgrim because of a Baroque façade that shields it from the elements.

As they do today, pilgrims knelt to greet the apostle, placing their hand in a niche in the stone, moulded by the hands of many before them. Pilgrims approached the resplendently adorned altar to embrace the painted figure of their saint and to whisper their petitions and kiss the displayed relics. Some

September: pilgrims returning from Santiago de Compostela, from the Hours of the Duchess of Burgundy (*c.* 1450). *Musée Condé, Chantilly, France/Bridgeman Art Library*

time after the twelfth century the relics were moved to a position under the main altar. Today, the pilgrim can visit St James's remains in the crypt where they are preserved in a silver reliquary. Pilgrims may also attend a communion to celebrate the completion of their journey. If one is timely enough to arrive on 25 July, the feast day of St James, or on another holy day, the spectacular swinging of the giant censer from floor to vaults is not to be missed, permeating the cathedral with an ethereal haze of incense.

The usual practice of settling in the cathedral to offer up prayers and to attend mass would follow the kissing of the relics. Having completed their journey, the medieval pilgrims could now implore the saint and make their requests for good harvests, cures from sickness, the health of their children, and so on. Today many choose to leave their requests to St James on pieces of paper, a more reserved approach perhaps more representative of Christian practice today.

An equally important part of a pilgrim's visit to a holy shrine was the offering of gifts and treasures. At Santiago de Compostela, this appears to have been a closely guarded operation wherein only cash and jewellery were accepted, deterring those pilgrims who had hoped their gifts of wood or lead would suffice.

The parish church of SS Mary and David, Kilpeck, Herefordshire. Inspired by Oliver de Merlimond's church of Shobdan, built on his return from a Compostela pilgrimage. Hugh of Kilpeck employed the same builders for his church of Kilpeck. *Sarah Hopper*

Having gone through the correct devotional procedures and visited the tomb of St James, the pilgrim could then seek to receive the plenary indulgence promised to all who made the journey, as well as permission to rest at Compostela for a further three days and nights. The pilgrim would then hope to find accommodation at one of the many hostelries in the city. Today if the pilgrim visits the Dean's House a 'Compostela' can be obtained as a certificate of proof that he has completed the journey and carried out his religious duties there.

For some pilgrims to Galicia, their journey was not felt to be complete until a further two- to three-day journey to Finisterre had been made. Fifty miles west of Santiago, this site was proclaimed as the 'End of the World' in medieval times. Its location offers stunning views across the Atlantic Ocean.

Despite a lack of written evidence that St James was ever in Spain during his lifetime or afterwards, his enduring significance as the inspiration and calling for many pilgrims to Compostela cannot be underestimated. A closer examination of the Camino, the route to Compostela and its history also highlights its earlier pagan significance, and others hold that its path mirrors the celestial path of the Milky Way, hence it has been called *la voje ladee*. It has been suggested that the Camino was important to the Celts, as they saw the route's end as the setting place of the sun, the ends of the earth. The floral motif that occurs in the medieval churches along the route has also been reinterpreted by some as an image of the sun.

For the pilgrims that reached Santiago de Compostela, a momentous and rewarding accomplishment of temporal and spiritual significance had been achieved. For many though, it was felt that the real journey only began with the uncertain trek home.

CHAPTER FIVE

THE LEGACY OF THOMAS BECKET: CANTERBURY

Where God, through his merits, wrought many miracles, where rich and poor, Kings and Princes, worshipped him, from whence the sound of his praise went forth into all the world.[1]

Thomas was the son of Gilbert and Matilda Becket, both Normans. He was born four days before Christmas Day in 1118 in Cheapside, London, and for many years he was known simply as Thomas of London. At the age of ten Thomas was sent to St Mary's in Merton, Surrey, to be educated by its Prior, Robert. He also enjoyed further education in Paris under his tutor Robert of Melun. Later, when he was archbishop of Canterbury, Thomas was to express his gratitude to both men. He made Robert of Merton his chaplain and orchestrated the ordination of Robert of Melun as Bishop of Hereford.

Before Thomas became archbishop, his father used his contacts to secure his son a place with the then archbishop, Theobald. Evidence suggests that Theobald had a great liking for the young Thomas, who was graced with a charm, energy and vitality, qualities that he greatly admired, but that could incite jealousy among others. Thomas's success and intelligence saw him sent abroad, this time in minor orders and to study law.

One of the fundamental advances in Thomas's career was when he journeyed to France and met the ailing King Stephen of England, who appointed Thomas chancellor to his heir, Henry II. This role would allow Thomas greater influence over matters concerning the Church than ever before, which delighted Archbishop Theobald.

Thomas was now mainly under the instruction of Henry II, fifteen years his junior. Much has been written on the stark differences that existed between the two men, as a precursor to the contentious feud that followed. Thomas was calm, handsome, shrewd as well as intelligent and business-minded. Whereas Henry was of a much coarser physique, restless, lecherous, and his red hair, associated with a fiery temper, was suitably fitting. He also suffered from the ability to bear an unrelenting grudge against anyone who displeased him.

In spite of this, the two men initially formed a strong friendship based on mutual respect. Henry recognised the experience and aptitude of his elder and Thomas the

vivacity and spirit of the young king. Thomas was fervently loyal and devoted to Henry to the point that some questioned his motives. To some it seemed that the archbishop had his own private agenda to persue. Equally, men of the Church began to fear that Thomas sought to strengthen the king at the expense of the Church. As a result of this and some independent views that Thomas chose to hold that displeased the Church, his close links with Theobald declined. On his deathbed Theobald asked for Thomas to come back to England to see him, but Thomas never came. Nonetheless, Theobald declared Thomas as his successor.

Henry appeared keen for Thomas to fill this role, although Thomas had quickly recognised the implications of becoming archbishop. This new role would reinforce the differences between himself and the king more firmly than ever before, and the

Opposite: St Thomas enthroned, stained glass, Canterbury Cathedral. *Sonia Halliday Picture Library*

A medieval map of Canterbury. *Sloane MS 2596. British Library/Bridgeman Art Library*

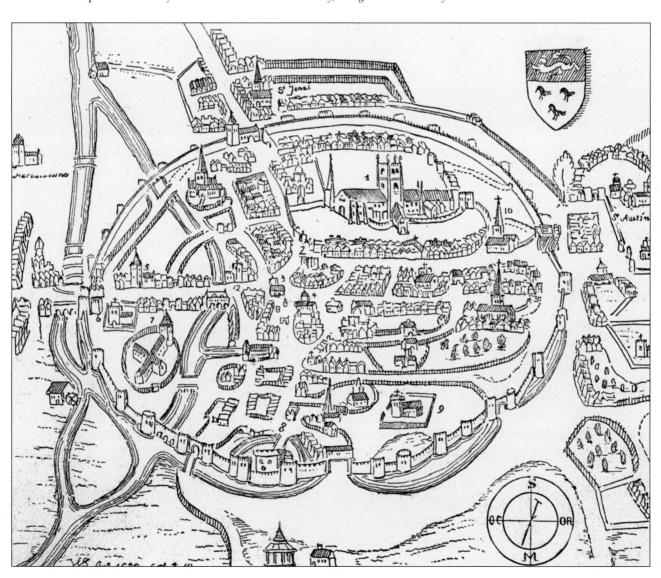

differing objectives of Church and State would be set in stone. Nonetheless, with candor and diplomacy Thomas's commitment to Henry never wavered. It was not long, though, before Henry began to recognise the potential problems and allowed himself to believe that Thomas was plotting to oppose him. Such notions were fuelled by gossipmongers and troublemakers. The divide between archbishop and king became ever wider as their opposing motives and desires for the directions of church and state were brought to the fore.

In an ostentatious assertion of his power, Henry called Thomas to a council meeting at Northampton at which he brought several charges against him. Many of these were unrelated to their main issues of contention, and yet Thomas was forced to answer them. As he left Northampton, Thomas was verbally and

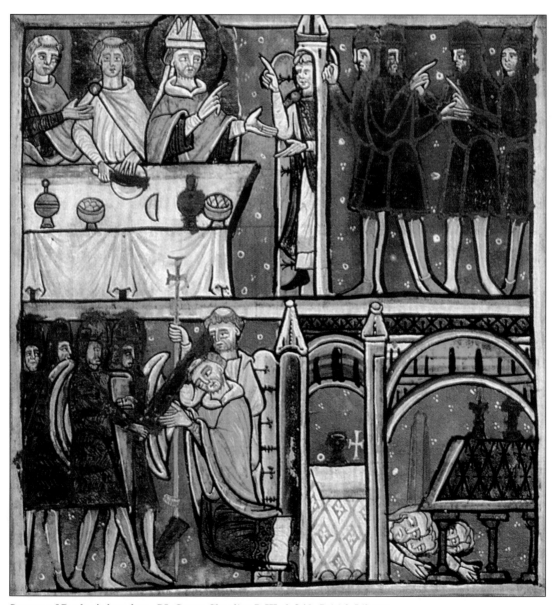

Scenes of Becket's last days, *BL Cotton Claudius B.III, f. 341. British Library*

physically attacked by the king's barons while, simultaneously, he became the champion of many lay people who saw him as their means of allaying the oppression of the monarchy. By now, though, many among the Church had deserted Becket, and he was forced to write to the Pope of his persecution. Becket escaped from England to France, an exile that lasted for six years. King Henry made no attempt to dissuade him and in Thomas's absence ordered the capture of all those relatives of Becket, as well as the relatives of Becket's colleagues, and all Canterbury's revenues were seized.

Becket wrote three letters to Henry in an effort to appease the situation, for which he received no reply. Eventually, though, a meeting was arranged between them, but it was called to an abrupt end with a customary outburst of rage by the king. Finally, with the intervention of the Pope, Henry and Becket succeeded in having a more peaceable meeting at which they talked and discussed their differences. Becket's position as archbishop of Canterbury was restored and he was encouraged by the king to return to England. Becket returned and his ravaged land and property were restored to him. He received a whole-hearted welcome on his arrival at Sandwich and was received warmly by all at Canterbury.

However, Becket was continually taunted by the king's belligerent barons. He seemed to have some insight into his impending death and became ever more vigilant in his prayers, alms-giving and acts of penance, including the wearing of a hair shirt. He also prophesied to a gathered congregation that Canterbury would soon experience another martyr. He then ordered the excommunication of many of the Churchmen who had opposed him, as well as Ranulf de Broc.

Meanwhile, such men sought to stir the anger of the king in order to seek their revenge. It is not certain what the exact words of the king were, but they were interpreted by four of his knights, Reginald Fitz-Urse, William de Tracy, Hugh de Moreville and Richard le Bret, as a clear order for the murder of Becket.

The knights arrived at Canterbury Cathedral at about 3 p.m. on 29 December 1170 in civil dress with their armour concealed. They brought with them a large retinue to ensure that they were prepared for any event. Fitz-Urse asked Becket, who was eating at table, if he would hear their business in public or private. Initially, Becket chose to meet the men in private, but a second assessment of his situation saw him recall his household. At first, the knights instructed Becket to absolve the bishops he had excommunicated and then go before the king to apologise for his past errors. Becket was resolute and would not oblige.

After much vociferation, Becket was confronted by the armed knights. Deserted but for one man, a clerk named Edward Grim, Becket remained calm and reticent, ready for the fate that was to befall him. He did attempt to defend himself as they attacked him, managing to throw one of them aside, but as they launched upon him with blows of their swords, Becket fell short. The third blow drove him to his knees, the fourth shattering the sword and slicing away the top of Becket's crown so that his brains spilled on to the cold floor. The knights then left the body of Becket where it fell and continued to ransack the rest of the cathedral. Henry II was said to have wept uncontrollably for three days.

Two days after the martyrdom, a woman in Sussex heard of the murder, prayed to the martyr and was cured. Shortly after this, a similar claim was made by a girl in Gloucester and then a day later by a knight in Berkshire. The Becket cult had begun.

Scenes from the Becket miracle windows, Trinity Chapel, Canterbury Cathedral. *John Crook*

A stone sarcophagus held the body of Becket in the crypt of Canterbury Cathedral and a large marble protective covering was placed over it. Two large, circular niches allowed the pilgrims to reach inside and touch the sarcophagus inside. Steadily the crowds visiting the tomb increased until on 21 February 1172, Becket was canonised, endorsing the enduring and effectual cult of St Thomas.

For those pilgrims arriving at the shrine within four years of Becket's death in 1170, their experience of the cathedral was an ordered affair. On entering, they would be greeted by one of the monks who would act as their guide on a structured tour and led to the first of the pilgrimage stations. This was in the north transept at the spot where Becket was slain. A column was removed and an altar placed to mark the spot at which pilgrims could see two shards of steel that had shattered from the sword of Richard le Bret as it smashed on the stone floor, a direct reminder to pilgrims of the ferocious nature of Becket's end. Inaccurate scenes of the martyrdom have depicted Becket kneeling at this altar at the time of his murder. Not only had the altar not been built yet, but on the afternoon the knights arrived, Becket had been dining with his brethren.

Pilgrims would then proceed up the steps, some on their knees, to the high altar where Becket's body was left to rest on the night of his murder. The next station took them down to the crypt. In the sombre stillness of the undercroft, pilgrims would behold the raised marble tomb.

Having been to the pilgrimage stations and attended mass, no pilgrim would wish to be without his own keepsake and reminder of the curative power of St Thomas. Having seen the saint depicted as a divine healer in the stained-glass miracle windows, pilgrims would go eagerly to fill their lead ampullae at the Well of St Thomas. Originally held to be the place at which Thomas had drunk each day,

Scenes from the twelfth-century Becket miracle windows in the Trinity Chapel, Canterbury Cathedral. *John Crook*

a reddish tinge of the water was later noted upon and attributed to the blood of the martyrdom imparted there by the monks. All traces of this well have now disappeared.

The miracle windows' portrayals of Thomas's many remedial interventions are ingenuously and strikingly conveyed. In one instance, Eilward of Westoning is shown sentenced to an unjust penalty and his eyes put out. St Thomas appears to him while he is in his bed and is shown holding two short staffs to Eilward's eyes. In the next scene, Eilward is shown with his sight fully restored, stooping in homage at Becket's shrine. In another episode, Hugh of Jervaulx is shown lying in bed with blood pouring from his nose. The inscription reads that as he drank of the water of St Thomas he was cured. Again, the episode concludes with Hugh dutifully giving thanks for his deliverance at Becket's tomb. Other anecdotes follow a similar pattern, such as the cripple having his foot bathed. The inscription tells us that again, as he made his vow and drank the blood, the swelling dissipated. Often St Thomas is shown appearing in a vision or dream of those who claimed that they were cured of their ailments. One scene in particular shows a sleeping man in the foreground, while over him hovers the figure of Thomas with cross nimbus, chasuble and cross as he emerges from his golden house shrine.[2]

On 5 September 1174 a fire destroyed the choir. This meant that pilgrims could not get to all the sites of Becket's martyrdom because of the building and repair work that had to be undertaken. However, an enlargement of the cathedral coincided with the construction of a new, raised chapel behind the high altar, purpose-built for the tomb of St Thomas. Archbishop Stephen Langton had declared it a far more appropriate and estimable location for the shrine of so prestigious a saint. The site was apparently chosen for its associations with St Thomas, as explained by Gervase, a contem-porary monk at Canterbury.

A Canterbury pilgrim badge of St Thomas.
Museum of London

> At the East end, also, he (William the
> Englishman) laid the foundation of the
> Chapel of the Holy Trinity, where
> St Thomas first solemnized mass, and used
> to indulge himself in tears and prayers.[3]

Gervase also states that the judicious nature of this setting was at the head of the cathedral. The stained glass in the Trinity chapel is aptly devoted to the many holy miracles credited to St Thomas. At the far east end is the Corona chapel, built to exhibit the thin portion of skull sliced from Becket's crown once on display there.

On 7 July 1220 was marked the important occasion of this translation of Thomas's bones. Resurrected from the crypt by Archbishop Stephen Langton, and witnessed by Henry II

The Trinity chapel, Canterbury Cathedral, showing the original site of Becket's shrine (marked by a candle) and the entrance to the Corona chapel on the right. *John Crook*

and a host of bishops and abbots, the relics were placed in majesty in a gold-plated chest. This was laid on a pink marble, arcaded pedestal, some six feet high, complete with a cover that could be raised on pulleys. A similar arrangement for the raising of a tomb's canopy is inferred in a depiction of that of St Edmund. Becket's shrine was richly adorned with gifts, most notably the *Régale de France*, a brilliant red ruby from Louis VII of France. Edward I later left the gold crown of Scotland as his offering. It is written that twenty-six wagons were required to transport the treasures away when Henry VIII destroyed the shrine in September 1538.

Today, one can observe part of the original, inlaid floor where the shrine stood and trace the ascending, easterly course leading to its original location at the cathedral's highest level. The ascent of the path towards the shrine was symbolic for the pilgrim. Accepting the symbolic nature of the shrine's prestigious location at the highest level of the cathedral, the following of this course was enacted as a kind of localised, spiritual journey. In a similar way to the Christological tours of the Holy Land, pilgrims were reliving Becket's last moments and retracing his steps. In climbing the steps towards the shrine, the pilgrim also raised his thoughts to a higher spiritual level, culminating with the sight of the dramatic shrine at the summit of his journey. Many sites required pilgrims to take confession before witnessing a holy shrine as a means of mentally and spiritually preparing them for the sanctity of what they were about to behold.

The shrine of St Thomas was guarded day and night. A considerable number of miracles were logged by two Canterbury monks, William and Benedict. Benedict, Prior of Canterbury in 1175, began recording the miracles chronologically a year after the martyrdom. William, another Canterbury monk, started recording in the following year, registering 438 miracles during the period 1172–79. Between them, Benedict and William chronicled 703 miracles in the first 10 years after Becket's death.

In the fifteenth century John Vyel and Edmund Kyngyston were two monks assigned with the office of guardians of the shrine. Their account of their duties at the shrine, written in Latin, has survived. One spiritual and one temporal guardian were required at the shrine, assisted by two lay clerks. The guardians were required to sleep within the shrine's precincts rising at 6 a.m. in winter and 5 a.m. in the summer, habitual rising hours which made the most of the natural light.[4]

The spiritual guardian would be charged with the celebration of daily mass at the shrine's altar, summoning pilgrims through the ringing of a bell. The guardians would also attend to the physical welfare of pilgrims; those who arrived suffering from heat and exhaustion would be offered refreshment and given bread. After the monastery's daily mass, the doors of the shrine precincts were closed to the public and an assistant clerk would have to seek out any stray dogs, thieves or lingering pilgrims.

Each Tuesday of the week was especially venerated in dedication to the martyr as the day of his death. The Feast of the Translation of Becket began each year on 7 July and lasted fifteen days until 21 July. The arrangements made for such veneration, the night vigils, masses and feasts in his honour would have required coordination as well as funding, for example for the perpetually burning candles placed around the shrine. Evidence certainly indicates the orderly and well-observed commitment required for the shrine's numinous and physical maintenance. For example, each year a thousand weight and three and a half hundred weight of wax was transported from London to Faversham and then overland to Canterbury for the sacristy alone.

Canterbury cathedral also received offerings of gifts and money, known as *oblaciones*. Some contemporary copies of treasurer's rolls have been preserved at Canterbury from which we can discern trends in the annual sums accumulated. For example, the jubilee years which marked the anniversary of Becket's martyrdom every fifty years saw greater sums being recorded. The first jubilee in 1220 (which also saw the Translation of Becket's bones to a new shrine) collected the staggering

John Lydgate and the Canterbury Pilgrims leaving Canterbury from *Troy Book and the Siege of Thebes*, 1412–22. *British Library/Bridgeman Art Library*

sum of £1,142 5s. This sum was chiefly made up from offerings to Becket's shrine and the site of the martyrdom. At this stage no mention is made of the Corona chapel where the fragment of Becket's skull was later preserved. Thereafter, though, offerings are noted as being made *ad caput Thomae* and *ad Coronam*, in other words to the Corona chapel and to its relic. The two years following saw a total of £151 20s offered here and in 1314 the sum of £115 12s was expended on the embellishment of the relic with gold and precious stones. This evidence would suggest that in the first jubilee year, the Corona chapel had not yet been completed, but by the year of the third jubilee, the fragment of Thomas's crown had been encased in what was most likely a head-shaped reliquary, on which pecuniary offerings were bestowed.

Other factors of a political or social nature served to influence pilgrim custom and the fluctuation of such figures. For example, the cathedral's hosting of the funeral of the Black Prince in 1376 and the crowning of King John and Queen Isabella saw peak years in nummular accounts. Equally, in the mid-fourteenth century, when the Black Death was at its most malignant, the shrine of Saint Thomas the healer witnessed exceptionally liberal offerings, as did the shrine of St Mary in the undercroft, which had previously seen leaner days in the shadow of the Becket phenomenon.

At its apogee in the last third of the fourteenth century, Christ Church, Canterbury, collected generous offerings at its high altar, tomb, site of the martyrdom, the Corona chapel and of course the shrine itself. Though such an income did not always balance out the cathedral's expenditure. With the progression of the fifteenth century and the outspoken teachings of those that questioned the fabric of the Church's teaching, the efficacy of holy relics, even pilgrimage, the Becket cult began to witness its own decline.

In 1420, the year of the popularly attended fifth jubilee, Christ Church also suffered the humiliation of an audit, by order of the Pope. Archbishop Chichele's unsanctioned dispensation of indulgences had been noted and the cathedral's records came under scrutiny. By 1532, a note in one of the sacrist's books recorded that the combined offerings at the cathedral amounted to £13 13s 3d, approximately thirty times less than that received by the shrine at the height of pilgrimage activity. Six years later, Henry VIII was to oversee the destruction of the shrine and the seizure of its vestiges and gifts.[5]

CHAPTER SIX

OUR LADY OF NORFOLK AND OTHER ENGLISH VENUES OF PILGRIMAGE

Therefore blessed Lady, grant thou thy great grace
To all that thee devoutedly visit in this place.[1]

The remarkable story of the unassuming village of Walsingham, near the north coast of Norfolk, began with a dream. A wealthy widow, Richeldis de Faverches, reported a vision in which the Virgin Mary appeared to her. The Virgin took her on a journey to the house in Nazareth where the Anunciation had taken place, the home in which Jesus had lived and been brought up. The Virgin's motives for this divine apparition became apparent when she prompted Richeldis to make a mental note of the building's dimensions, and to build a complete replica of the Holy House in Norfolk.

The notion that such a large undertaking as this could be prompted by an isolated reverie was not exceptional to the medieval mind. Many divine insights, miracle cures and saintly visitations occurred through visions or dreams. Similarly, other religious buildings owed their construction to the promptings of a dream, such as the Basilica of Santa Maria Maggiore in Rome. Similarly, when Abbot Hugh of Cluny, in the eleventh century, decided to begin the third building of the abbey church there, it is written in the *Chronicon Cluniacense* that one of his monks, Gonzo, was lying sick in bed, when SS Peter and Paul visited him in a dream and with the aid of lengths of rope, showed him the dimensions and shape of the church to be built.

The divine direction in the construction of the holy house at Walsingham was set to continue. It seems that there was some indecision as to the best location for the house until a miraculous occurrence one morning. Curiously, two areas of ground had been left untouched by the morning dew. Richeldis happily ordered the village craftsmen and workmen to begin construction between these markers. Strangely, though, the construction would not hold safely to the foundations. Again, this was interpreted as a divine omen and the construction was relocated.

Once the holy house was complete, its divine significance was sanctioned by the supernatural dream that had seen its making, as well as the notion that the holy Virgin was so taken with the building as to relocate from her spiritual resting place in Nazareth to reside in Norfolk. This saw the beginning of Walsingham's certain

Remains in the Abbey grounds at Walsingham include a large Norman arch. *Sarah Hopper*

The Lady Chapel, Walsingham. *John Crook*

future as a celebrated site on the pilgrim itinerary; from the year 1061 Walsingham
came to be revered as 'England's Nazareth'.

As a precursor to the events of the Dissolution of the monasteries, one sceptic was
quick to try to dispel the supernatural charm of Walsingham. On his visit in 1512,
the humanist scholar Erasmus reported 'the church is graceful and elegant; but the
Virgin does not occupy it.'[2] He also portrayed a rather inelegant image of the house,
not befitting such a prestigious resident. He complains of the bitter drafts that blew
through open doors and windows, associating these with the house's proximity to
the sea.

Perhaps to compensate for the less forgiving British weather compared to that of
Nazareth, Walsingham's wooden replica was encased within a stone church, roughly
twenty-three by thirteen feet. Crusaders returning from the Holy Land later
presented the shrine with a holy relic. Pilgrims could now cast their eyes over a
sample of holy milk from the Virgin's breast, curiously captured in a phial. However,
not all were so easily taken in. On beholding the phial, Erasmus described its
content as an unappealing congealed mess, like 'ground chalk, mixed with the
white of egg!'[3]

Anxious that a religious order be founded in order to maintain the shrine, on leaving
for crusade, Richeldis's son Geoffrey left instruction with his clerk. In about 1153,

The ruins of Castle Acre Priory. *Sarah Hopper*

Augustinian canons established a priory next to the holy house, now partly constituted by the Bull public house. Two centuries later, in 1347, a rival Franciscan friary was established. Walsingham's quiet, unassuming days as a little-known backwater were fast over as it became a focal point for pilgrims all over Britain and Europe.

The face of the village was irretrievably transformed as new accommodation and hostelries were built to cater for its eager visitors, and the village's meandering lanes assumed a reorganised grid system. For the modern visitor, Little Walsingham still offers much that is reminiscent of its days as a famed pilgrimage spot, and indeed it continues to operate as such. Many of the timber-framed, jettied buildings still stand, and the 'holy mile', the last leg of the journey along the River Stiffkey from Houghton St Giles to Little Walsingham, is still trod by pilgrims today. The Holy House itself, as the faithful heart of the village, still radiates its pious message drawing pilgrim and politician alike to contemplate its enduring significance.

Nearby King's Lynn to the west or Wells-next-the-sea on the north coast provided convenient ports for the arrival of foreign pilgrims, and some surrounding villages still bear evidence of having housed the pilgrim. It seems likely that some, most likely those pilgrims landing on the north coast, may have found rest at the priory at Binham, just north-east of Walsingham; its village green still hosts a wayside cross. Flitcham and Castle Acre also seem probable villages for the hostelry of pilgrims.

The wayside chapels lining the many routes, allowing pilgrims to attend to their pious duties along the way, are also significant. At King's Lynn, there still exists the intriguing Red Mount chapel, dating from 1485. Dedicated to St Mary, it takes the form of a red-brick, octagonal turret. Positioned on a hill mound, it housed a vestry and three separate chapels, one of which was for pilgrims. King's Lynn was also the home of Margery Kempe, who dictated the earliest surviving autobiography in English which describes her personal desperation, orthodox piety and agreement with her husband that she should go off on a pilgrimage. Leaving King's Lynn, she travelled as far as the Holy Land, arriving there in 1414. On returning from her second pilgrimage, this time to Santiago de Compostela, she describes how she walked from Dover to London wearing sackcloth and moralising to Londoners on their less than virtuous city behaviour!

South of the shrine at Little Walsingham is the Slipper chapel of Houghton St Giles. This served as a wayside chapel for pilgrims where they could offer their devotions and give thanks for safe passage before reaching their destination a mile away. It is called the Slipper chapel as pilgrims would remove their shoes here out of devotion and walk the last stretch of their journey barefoot. Thomas Becket had walked barefoot when he caught his first welcome glimpse of Canterbury cathedral on returning from exile. In the 1930s, the Slipper chapel was revived and now exists as the Roman Catholic shrine to Our Lady, still welcoming many thousands of pilgrims each year.

On arrival at Walsingham, the pilgrim was greeted with the usual scene of a busy main street lined with inns and tradesmen. On entering the gates of the priory pilgrims were led into a small chapel dedicated to St Lawrence wherein they would be invited to kiss a holy relic, the purported fingerbone of St Peter. Walsingham also offered the sick pilgrim the opportunity to bathe in the cool waters of its healing bath. Sheltered by a thatched roof, there were also two holy wells, the water of which was purported to cure headaches and stomach pains, as well as granting wishes.

The Chapel of the Holy Spirit, Walsingham. *Sarah Hopper*

The operation was overseen by guardian monks who supervised the bathing of those who carried a valid note from their physician. They also facilitated those who came to cast their wish to the power of the holy wells. After the Reformation, the wells managed to retain their custom, supposedly granting only the wishes of those who refrained from uttering their request aloud for the year following. Many pilgrims also chose to take away samples of Walsingham's holy water in small lead flasks or ampoules. These usually had the letter 'W' stamped on them to show that they came from Walsingham.

St Winifred's Well at Holywell offered a similar service for pilgrims who came seeking the curative compassion of this saint. Legend states that early in the seventh century a pious young woman in North Wales was decapitated by Prince Caradoc. Her head rolled through the doorway of the church where the congregation were assembled and St Beuno, as he became, reunited it with her body and managed to revive her to perfect health. At the spot at which she had first fallen, a healing well burst forth accompanied by a sweet redolence. The star-shaped well came to be housed within a vault with a processional ambulatory for the passage of pilgrims. A surviving carving shows a sick pilgrim being carried down the steps to the well. On acquisition of Winifred's relics in the twelfth century, the religious house at Shrewsbury also became a marked site of pilgrimage.

Having bathed in Walsingham's curative waters, pilgrims would next pass through a narrow wicker gate called the Knight's Gate, and were thus reminded of the miraculous powers of Our Lady of Walsingham. Over it, the gate once carried a plaque showing a knight on horseback, Sir Ralph Boutetout. In 1314 Boutetout was racing to sanctuary within the holy house at Walsingham with his enemy hot on his heels. Arriving at the narrow gate, he quickly realised that seated high on his horse and protected from head to toe in heavy armour, the gate was too small to let him in. Legend states that one invocation to Our Lady of Walsingham saw him gliding swiftly through the gate to safety. Among the designs for Walsingham pilgrim badges showing the Anunciation and the Virgin in the Holy House is another depicting Sir Ralph mounted on his steed and framed by his gate.

Once through the Knight's Gate, the goal of the pilgrim's journey was in clear view. Inside the wooden house, pilgrims were able to behold the celebrated statue of the Virgin, seated on a throne with the infant Jesus on her knee and holding a lily sceptre, a symbol of peace, as depicted in the priory seal. Having seen the phial of the Virgin's milk in the priory church and offered the appropriate prayers and incantations, the pilgrim would then be able to receive his forty-day indulgence.

Being a smaller, narrower venue unlike the grand cathedrals of Canterbury or Compostela, the priory had to make special compensatory arrangements for its pilgrim visitors. The Holy House had a door open on each side to allow the single, one-way passage of traffic through the house, and as soon as pilgrim offerings were

The bath and twin wells, Walsingham. *Sarah Hopper*

left at the shrine, they were hastily gathered up to prevent theft. Erasmus describes the feelings of discomfort induced by the ever vigilant watch of the convent's members, as if 'some sacrilegious thief had pilfered something from the ornaments of the Holy Virgin, and that some suspicion had fallen on me.'[4] He also disclosed the greater impulse among pilgrims to leave gifts at the shrine if they felt they were being watched by the attendants, as well as to give more generously than they normally would. This seemed to emanate from a kind of pious guilt and shame, perhaps the same sentiment that spurred many to go on pilgrimage in the first place.

Not surprisingly, with the Dissolution under Henry VIII, Walsingham saw sad times. Bishop Latimer's letter to Thomas Cromwell in the sixteenth century expressed his resounding distaste at the devotion focused on the shrines of the Virgin at Walsingham, Ipswich and others. Their statues of the Virgin were taken to Chelsea in London, and ceremonially burned. A lament survives from the papers of the Earl of Arundel, who died in the Tower in 1595 at the command of Elizabeth I. His words must surely have reflected the thoughts and sentiments of all those that had travelled the distance to this remote village in Norfolk.

> Bitter, bitter, oh to behold the grass to grow,
> Where the walls of Walsingham so stately did show
> Level, Level with the ground the towers do lie
> Which with their golden glittering tops pierced once to the sky.[5]

Happily, Walsingham's prestige as a popular attraction was restored in the 1930s when, under its vicar, Alfred Hope Patten, a replica of the Holy House was re-created now existing as an Anglican shrine. Today the shrine's religious calendar includes an annual national pilgrimage held on Spring Bank Holiday Monday, as well as the annual reception of Peers and MPs who arrive to offer their devotions.

Among the concentration of shrines to the north-west of London were Worcester, Hailes, Gloucester and Hereford. Worcester cathedral housed the shrines of two saints, St Oswald and St Wulstan. Bishop Oswald had founded a Benedictine monastery at Worcester in 964. In 1041, the monastery was burnt down by the Danes and the images and shrines of its saints and their bones were destroyed. As Bishop of Worcester and Archbishop of York, Oswald was able to recover the relics of Saxon saints at the derelict minster at Ripon. He housed them at Worcester cathedral in a silver reliquary. After Oswald's death in 992 and canonisation a decade later, his tomb was opened and his own bones transferred to the same reliquary.

Later, in 1089, Wulstan, by then prior and bishop of Worcester, completed the first stage of a new cathedral and translated the shrine of his predecessor to the new building. He also further embellished the reliquary, spending the considerable amount of 72 marks of silver. Wulstan died in about 1095 and was placed in his own tomb. As the oldest surviving Saxon bishop who had managed to hold off subjugation by the Norman conquerors, he also was canonised.

The tombs of both bishops acquired a great reputation and respect throughout the Middle Ages. King John requested that he be enshrined between the tombs of Oswald and Wulstan after his death, the notion being that these two venerated saints would be able to assist him on his own journey through purgatory. King John's tomb in Worcester cathedral carries little figures of the two saints, one on each side of his effigy.

The tomb of King John in Worcester Cathedral. His effigy is flanked by SS Oswald and Wulstan. *John Crook*

Miracles at the tomb of St Wulstan were being reported by pilgrims from an early stage and were recorded in the thirteenth-century collection, *Miraculi Wulstani*, or the Miracles of Wulstan. This record also recounts the techniques employed at the shrine to exorcise demons, their ideas being logical in a medieval sense, if not cruel. In order to make the body a less inviting and comfortable residence for the demon, the subject would be hit and beaten, with other pilgrims often invited to join in. One boy claimed that he saw a demon leave his body and shake an angry fist at the tomb of St Wulstan before departing!

Holy water associated with St Wulstan, or 'Wulstan's Water' was sought after by visiting pilgrims for curative reasons. Much diluted, it was put into lead ampoules stamped with names and images of St Mary and St Wulstan, becoming the main token associated with the shrine. Today Worcester cathedral still boasts the remains of its Guesten Hall, originally built in 1320 to accommodate its visiting pilgrims.

In Gloucestershire, pilgrims could visit the tomb of Edward II in Gloucester cathedral, as well as the prestigious relic held by Hailes Abbey, the holy blood of

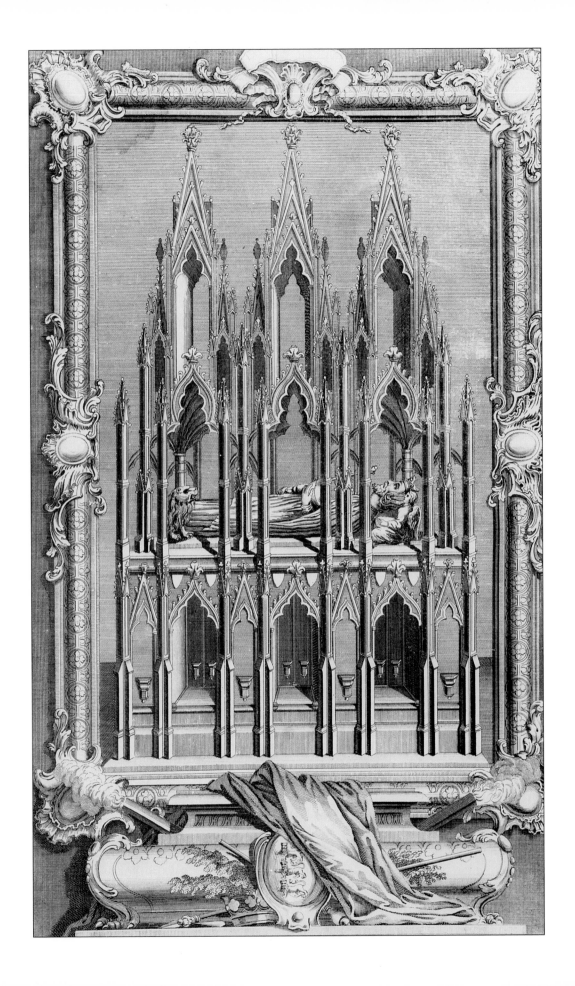

Christ caught in a glass phial. As with Becket, greater sanctity was attached to the shrine of Edward II on account of his particularly violent end. Kept captive by his successors, allies of Queen Isabella, Edward II was eventually murdered at Berkeley Castle in 1327. A wave of anger and emotion swept England and the Abbot of St Peter's at Gloucester rescued the king's corpse and had it buried in the north aisle of the cathedral. The tomb was a grand expression of devotion and veneration with angels supporting the head of the king's effigy and a lion at his feet. Dating to about 1340, it is also noteworthy for its use of alabaster, as well as its especially ornate limestone canopy.

In spite of the Pope's rejection of requests to canonise Edward, his posthumous veneration continued. Between 1337 and 1350, Edward III ordered the rebuilding of the cathedral's choir in which his father's shrine was placed, partly facilitated by the offerings of visiting pilgrims.

The tomb of an earlier king of England resided in Westminster Abbey. The Bayeux Tapestry gives us a wonderful depiction of the half-French king, Edward the Confessor. The beginning of the work shows the end of Edward's life. He is shown ailing and recumbent on his sickbed where he died on 5 January 1066. Also depicted is Westminster Abbey which was built in the Confessor's reign; the weathercock was put in position to announce its completion. The Confessor was buried before the high altar.

Again, from fairly early on, miracles were reported by those visiting the shrine. Edward the Confessor was heralded as a saint by the people, although he was not actually canonised until 1161. Perhaps the most intriguing story attached to the dead king was the ordered opening of the Confessor's tomb by Henry I in 1102. This was to satisfy a rumour that the late king's body lay untouched by natural decomposition. Bishop Gundulf of Rochester stood present as a witness to the unperished body and was rebuked for attempting to take some of Edward's beard back to Rochester as a holy relic!

St Cuthbert at Durham was another saint whose remains were reported to have remained intact after his death. The guardian of Cuthbert's shrine is said to have had the added duty of combing the saint's hair and trimming his nails, which continued to grow. Cuthbert's biographer, the venerable Bede, was also enshrined in Durham Cathedral.

In 1163, Thomas Becket was responsible for translating Edward the Confessor's remains into a new, magnificent shrine that had been built by Henry II in Westminster Abbey. Under Henry III, the remains were translated again, this time to a new shrine near the high altar. A large pedestal was created by piling up what was said to be earth brought back from the Holy Land. Not only did this raise the shrine to a level where everybody could see it, but there was greater reverence associated with the more elevated positioning of the shrine. This translation of the body on 13 October 1269 was a momentous occasion, and many came to leave their votive candles and offerings. For 300 years afterwards, Londoners celebrated this day as the Feast of the Translation of St Edward.

Hubert Gravelot's (1699–1773) engraving of the monument of Edward II in Gloucester Cathedral. *Private Collection/Bridgeman Art Library*

The feretory in Durham Cathedral looking west with a black slab marking the site of the shrine of St Cuthbert, now his grave. *John Crook*

Edward I, the Hammer of the Scots who came to the throne three years after the translation, made his own offerings to the shrine. These were a fragment of the True Cross encrusted with jewels, as well as the Stone of Destiny or Stone of Scone, as it is also known. This stone had been used by the Scots as the ceremonial seat on which their kings were crowned. Edward I had taken the stone to Westminster, and until 1996, when it was returned to Scotland, it resided underneath the Coronation Chair that was built to house it.

Today the shrine of St Edward in Westminster Abbey is no less of a visual delight in the Chapel of the Confessor. Its pedestal lifts the shrine seven feet clear of the ground and is host to inlaid red and green porphyry stone, gold and mosaic, all undertaken by a man called Petrus Romanus, or Peter the Roman. Pilgrims climbed through the trefoiled arches of the pedestal to get close to the shrine, make their offerings and ask the saint for help. Pilgrims probably went more to behold the wondrous sight of the Confessor's rich tomb than in quest of holy miracles. Equally, he came to be considered more a patron of the English monarchy than of the English people.

Undoubtedly, those pilgrims to the shrine of Edward II in Gloucester cathedral would also visit the Cistercian Abbey of Hailes about three miles away. There, a most distinguished, if not intriguing, relic was housed. Reputedly from a vase that had been enclosed in a leaden box and marked *Jesu Christi Sanguis*, this sample of Christ's blood fuelled much attention and enquiry among pilgrims and others. The box was said to have originated in Mantua in 804, which also produced a second phial in the garden of a hospice there nearly two and a half centuries later. In 1267, the founder of Hailes Abbey purchased a phial of the relic from the Count of Holland and brought it back to England, giving a third of it to Hailes. In the usual fashion, rebuilding and organising within the abbey was set underway to house

The ruins of Hailes Abbey. *John Crook*

the new relic, and a custodian was appointed to display it to pilgrims and receive their offerings.

Perhaps most closely related to the living essence of a venerated figure, relics constituted by blood, particularly that of Christ, were not unusual to the medieval pilgrim who could also witness such examples in Mantua, Normandy, Bruges and Rome. Nonetheless, some expressed scepticism as to the authenticity of such a relic and, while more readily accepting the recovery of other Christological objects such as the crown of thorns or the True Cross, questioned the practicalities of salvaging Christ's blood. Such doubts were often countered with the notion that those with access to Christ may have gathered the blood on any of the five occasions when he was reported to have shed it, for example at Calvary from his hands and feet, or the blood issued from his forehead by the crown of thorns, even that shed at Christ's circumcision. However, with the Dissolution Bishop Latimer and the commissioners examined the phial and declared it to be nothing like blood. With so many other vestiges of pilgrimage the holy blood of Hailes was consigned to the flames in London.

West of Hailes, the cathedral at Hereford was very popular with pilgrims, on account of its shrine to Hereford's former bishop, Thomas Cantilupe. When Cantilupe died of fever on his way to Rome in 1282, his chaplain, Richard Swinfield charged himself with the task of transporting the bishop's bones back to Hereford. He did this by boiling the corpse to separate the flesh from the bones and encasing the heart in a box. In 1287 the bones were laid to rest in the Lady Chapel of the cathedral at Hereford and Richard was pronounced bishop. Thomas Cantilupe is said to have been the last Englishman before the Reformation to be canonised, this occurring in 1320 on account of the many miracles transpiring at his tomb. In 1349, the monks of Hereford carried the relics through the streets at the height of the Black Death in an effort to stem its wake.

Part of the Cantilupe shrine, made from purbeck marble, can still be seen in the north transept of the cathedral today. Its beautiful arcaded canopy, intricately carved with leaf designs, rests on a carved base depicting fourteen Knights Templar, each housed within a trefoil arch. Thomas had served as a Grand Master.

Thomas Cantilupe's posthumous veneration placed Hereford firmly on the pilgrim circuit and brought many to be healed at the shrine, including one of Edward I's prized falcons, which was housed in a purpose-built cage with a fountain in a mews in Charing. When the bird fell sick, the king entrusted its health to St Thomas at Hereford where he placed a wax effigy of the bird along with his generous fiscal offering.

The city of York also had its own venerable saint, Archbishop William Fitzherbert from the twelfth century. His canonisation enabled York to announce its new status as a site of interest to the pilgrim. A ceremony at which Edward III and his queen were present saw the translation of the saint's bones to a shrine behind the altar. As at Canterbury, a pictorial commentary on the miracles of St William was commemorated in the stained glass, including an intriguing instance of a pilgrim who narrowly escaped death when a large stone fell on him.

Winchester venerated St Swithun, one of its earlier bishops from the ninth century. Winchester was already firmly marked on the map as it was a focus for tradesmen and travellers to Southampton, and it had been the capital of England in late Saxon times. As with Canterbury, it was also a productive artistic centre

The tomb of Bishop Thomas Cantilupe in Hereford Cathedral. *John Crook*

producing such manuscripts as the Winchester Bible with its beautiful historiated initials. Standing on the site of an older abbey church, its cathedral is of majestic proportions and a good example of Norman architectural expertise.

Long before the martyrdom of Thomas Becket in 1170, the shrine of St Swithun at Winchester was a popular destination for pilgrims. On his death in 862, Swithun had specifically requested to be buried in the common graveyard, open to the elements and the feet of passers-by. Nine years later on 15 July the cathedral monks attempted to move the body inside the cathedral, but their efforts were foiled by an impromptu downpour that lasted a further forty days and nights.

The Pilgrims' Hall on the south-west side of the cathedral was constructed to accommodate the large numbers of pilgrims hoping to be cured by St Swithun. With the martyrdom of Becket, pilgrims would follow the trail from Winchester through Farnham, Guildford, Reigate and Oxted on the way to Canterbury.

CHAPTER SEVEN

DRESSED AND BLESSED: PREPARING FOR THE JOURNEY

Reynard now sees that this is what he must do. He takes a scrip and staff and sets out on his way, looking every inch a pilgrim.[1]

Before going on a pilgrimage there were preparations to be made. Rudimentary arrangements demanded by an uncertain journey away from home included the settling of debts and bringing closure to any outstanding disputes. In her fifteenth-century account, Margery Kempe relates how she requested that her parish priest make an announcement to the congregation. If any there claimed any money owing from herself or her husband they should come to discuss it with her before she set off and she would endeavour to make payment. Equally important was the drawing up of a will; this was to include the naming of heirs, details of the purpose of one's trip, the intended length of time away and the places one planned to visit. In the likelihood that the pilgrim did not return a year and a day after the proposed date of return, his property and items listed would be handed to the named heirs.

There were also other obligatory procedures that would prepare the pilgrim spiritually and physically for the journey ahead. First, the pilgrim required the permission of his overlord, bishop or abbot, if he was a monk, in order to undertake the pilgrimage. If his journey was approved, he would be given a letter of commendation to be carried with him. This document was important for three reasons. First, it verified his purpose as a pious exercise so that he was not mistaken for a wanderer. Secondly, it made him eligible for the privileges to which a pilgrim was entitled while undertaking his journey, such as alms and lodgings. Lastly, it was a crucial symbol of his status as a pilgrim. Under an ordinance of Richard II in 1388, a pilgrim could be arrested if discovered without this letter of *testimoniales* on his person. This was partly to discourage the abuse of pilgrimage by adventurers of less than pious motives.

Opposite. The fresco of *The Pilgrim* by Nicolo and Stefano da Ferrara (after Giotto), *c.* 1450. *Palazzo della Ragione, Padua, Italy/Bridgeman Art Library*

Next, of fundamental importance was the receipt of the Church's blessing in a specially written consecration ceremony. This was followed by the ceremonial adornment of the subject in the recognised pilgrim's garb. This religious ceremony, which commended the pilgrim to God and to service as a pilgrim, was called the *ordo ad servitium peregrinorum*. The subject would be blessed along with each article of pilgrimage that would go with the pilgrim. The Sarum Missal, written between 1150 and 1319, included the mass and blessing to be performed for this purpose.

> The almighty and everlasting God, Who is the Way, the Truth, and the Life, dispose your journey according to His good pleasure; send his angel Raphael to keep you in this your pilgrimage, and both conduct you in peace on your way to the place where you would be, and bring you back again on your return to us in safety.[2]

Having attended confession to expiate the conscience of any remaining sin, the subject would then prostrate himself in front of the altar. With the congregation as his witness, masses would be said and finally, the subject's 'pilgrim status' would be conferred on him by way of the consecration of his scrip and staff, each sprinkled with holy water and correctly placed on his person. For those making the pilgrimage to Jerusalem, their cloak would also be adorned with a red cross at the shoulder.

The mass that followed this procedure would suitably reiterate biblical passages relevant to the practice of pilgrimage, for example Christ's words to his apostles in Matthew 10: 7–15,

> You have received without paying, so give without being paid. Do not carry any gold, silver or copper money in your pockets; do not carry a beggar's bag for the journey or an extra shirt or shoes or a stick. Workers should be given what they need. When you come to a town or village, go in and look for someone who is willing to welcome you, and stay with him until you leave that place.

The notion of travelling without worldly comforts and trusting that God would provide for your needs was one synonymous with the idea of a spiritual pilgrimage, although many efforts were made to ensure that the pilgrim would find food and shelter along the way. Pilgrims also travelled lightly, not least because it would have been otherwise impractical to make such journeys on foot.

Pilgrims would often be escorted to the city gates or just outside the town by members of the village, brotherhood or guild. Some guilds had particular rules concerning the undertaking of pilgrimage by one of their members, so that small donations of money would be made to their cause. The fourteenth-century Guild of the Resurrection, at Lincoln, encouraged its members to give at least a halfpenny to the departing pilgrim.[3] In this way, such guilds felt they were partaking in the virtue and merit of the pilgrimage. Some guilds went further by opening houses as lodging for the poor pious traveller.

Of the pilgrim attire, the staff played a fundamental role in the pilgrim's garb as a symbolic yet functional motif of pilgrimage that can be seen in the literature and art of the period. It is through these mediums that most evidence of the traditional pilgrim's dress can be found. The most common show the wearing of a long cloak over a tunic, not unlike the common dress in medieval England. However, items that made this outfit unique to the pilgrim were a pair of sturdy boots for walking, or as good quality as one could afford. Chaucer's monk chose expensive, soft leather for his comfort. A multifunctional broad-brimmed hat served not only to protect against exposure to the sun, but was also useful for displaying souvenir badges.

Brother Faber, the Dominican friar, relates that there were four outward signs that identified a pilgrim bound for the Holy Land. These were the red cross on a long grey gown, a black or grey hat with a red cross, a scrip and a long beard. If in the Holy Land, an ass replaced a staff. On foot though, a substantial walking staff, or 'bourdon' was a reliable companion, serving the dual purpose of support and, if necessary, defence. In an amusing citation on the use of pilgrim staffs, an unruly and impatient crowd of pilgrims on St Richard's Day in 1487 took to using their staffs on each other! The Bishop of Chichester was forced to impose new rules whereby only crosses and banners could be taken inside the cathedral. The staff often carried a single or double knob at the top, and most commonly a double-pronged, iron spike at the bottom, probably to grip the ground when climbing. Later versions of the bourdon had a hook at the top from which a water bottle could be suspended. The pilgrim would also carry a scrip, or leather satchel, usually suspended from a belt worn across the body. This would carry provisions and a water bottle, sometimes called a 'calabase', as well the important pilgrim's letter of safe conduct signed by the church authorities. Other small items of convenience could also carried in it. The scrip and staff became emblematic of pilgrimage and held personal significance for the pilgrim. On return they were cherished by the pilgrim as reminders of their great undertaking. Many pilgrims were buried with their scrips and staffs, such as the pilgrim found buried under the main tower of Worcester Cathedral. The wooden staff measured just over a metre and a half in height with a double-pronged wrought-iron spike at the bottom. Also lying close to the staff at the bottom of the grave was a scallop shell with a hole pierced at the top for wearing as a brooch, which would suggest that the pilgrim had been to Compostela. Scallops can be found from the south-west of England to the Iberian peninsula, as well as on the Mediterranean and Atlantic coast of Morocco, making it difficult to determine, exactly where he acquired his token.

The Worcester pilgrim was also buried wearing a well-preserved pair of knee-length leather boots, a style popular at the end of the fifteenth century. They also display the more practical, and, no doubt, more comfortable rounded toe that superseded the archetypal medieval pointed toe. The fact that the subject is buried in full pilgrim's garb opens various lines of enquiry. Did he die while on pilgrimage and was then buried at Worcester? Or perhaps he had kept his pilgrim's garb from a journey made before? The fact that both of his boots appear to have been slit along the top centre of each foot tends to suggest that they were placed on the feet after death. It is also possible of course that this man had never made a pilgrimage and that the nature of his burial symbolised an unfulfilled desire, even a vow to do so. Intriguing still, though, is the evidence of wear and tear to the staff and boots.

Anatomical evidence supporting the theory that this man died a pilgrim are the well developed shoulder muscles, more so on the right side, and there is also evidence of inflammation to the shoulder joint. Assuming that the pilgrim was right-handed (his staff was buried at his right side), this evidence could point to constant use of a staff and repeated lifting, throwing forward and pushing down on the right arm and shoulder. The heel of the right hand which would have incurred direct pressure from such a movement shows evidence of arthritis.

Pilgrims giving alms from *The Book of Good Morals*, Jacques le Grant, fifteenth century. *MS 297/1338.*
Musée Condé, Chantilly, France/Bridgeman Art Library

Perhaps most interesting is the evidence for prolonged hard use of the feet. The 'take-off' movement of the foot as we walk is largely dependent on a long tendon ending at the big toe. In the case of the Worcester pilgrim, this has formed a significant groove in the bone, much more so than normal.

Perhaps the most memorable and colourful images of the medieval pilgrim are Chaucer's party of fourteenth-century marauding revellers. Much less the portrayal of spiritual devotion and penitential journeying, Chaucer's pilgrims exhibit the very exuberance and revelry for which pilgrimage became targeted by the Church and others. Their dress also exhibits material rather than spiritual indulgence. Chaucer's pilgrims ride on horseback modelling a lavish display of grey fur, expensive soft leather, taffeta and silk, often richly decorated as in the case of the monk's 'ful curious pin' and the prioress' inappropriately elaborate rosary:

> A peire of bedes, gauded al with grene,
> And thereon heng a brooch of gold ful sheene,
> On which ther was first write a crowned A,
> And after AMOR VINCIT OMNIA.[4]

The Prioress, detail, from the *Canterbury Tales*, Ellesmere Manuscript, 1911. *Private Collection/ Bridgeman Art Library*

While the dying of cloth was a costly and dangerous business in the Middle Ages, involving the exporting and reimportation of cloth from the Netherlands, many of the brightest and most expensive colours are noted in the attire of Chaucer's merry band. The wife of Bath for example wears hose of 'fyn scarlet reed', the most expensive of colours and usually confined to the clothes of the nobility as a result. Of the doctor, 'In sangwin [scarlet] and in pers he clad was al', and of the bawdy miller, 'A white cote and a blew hood wered he'.[5]

Although widely popular, pilgrimage often involved lengthy, arduous journeys with many dangers on the way. Before leaving his home, the pilgrim would have had to put his affairs in order. For the majority, survival in medieval society depended on a strict regime of farm and domestic labours dictated by the months of the year. Surviving medieval books of hours offer us the best evidence and illustration of this. As well as outlining a daily regime of pious devotion, they often included a calendar illustrating the agricultural year.

January	Feasting
February	Warming by the fire
March	Pruning
April	Horticultural scenes
May	Hawking/boating
June	Hay harvest
July	Corn reaping
August	Threshing
September	Grape treading
October	Ploughing/sowing
November	Acorn gathering (for feeding swine)
December	Pig slaughtering/bread baking

Finding workers to assist in the upkeep of such a hefty schedule was but one of the many domestic concerns of the departing pilgrim and indeed must have prevented some from doing so. It is interesting to note therefore that apart from the obvious attraction of indulgences to lure a man away on pilgrimage, the later Middle Ages also saw judicial reforms that enabled the pilgrim to leave home with legal assurances that his domestic schedule would continue unimpaired in his absence.

There were other attractive benefits for those who chose to make the arduous journey to the Holy Land. The *licentia Romani pontificis*, which commended pilgrims to make this journey, also gave them certain benefits, such as they would be immune from any criminal or civil suits brought against them while on pilgrimage, stays against any such suits that involved debt, as well as access to special facilities for monetary loans.

Even in light of the above assurances, it is important to bear in mind the financial disadvantages of travel in Medieval times. Without the modern convenience of credit cards, traveller's cheques and banks as we know them, the pilgrim would

Opposite: October: ploughing and sowing, *Très Riches Heures du Duc de Berry. Musée Condé, Chantilly, France/Bridgeman Art Library*

generally have to raise sufficient funds up front to support his whole journey and carry it with him. He would also have to make allowance for the offerings and donations he would make at the many shrines along the way as well as have enough money to buy ampullae and tokens worn as talismans. Many pilgrims fell foul of thieves, among them fellow pilgrims, who sought to gain at the expense of another.

Faber, who made two journeys to the Holy Land, the first in 1480 and the second in 1483, shows what an undertaking pilgrimage could be. His promise to the brethren of the Dominican Convent of Ulm resulted in an exact record of everything he saw. His own fears before undertaking his pilgrimage must have reflected those of many. 'Moreover it was a serious matter for me to ask for leave for so long and so unusual a wandering, and it appeared to be almost impossible for me to obtain it. Nor could I form any idea of how I should raise the money for such an expensive journey.'[6]

While many pilgrims made their way by begging, some pilgrims were lucky enough to receive gifts of money for their journey. Edward III gave his messenger William Clerk the sum of £1, 6*s* and 8*d* for his pilgrimage to Jerusalem.[7]

In modern terms, the pilgrim's passport was his easily distinguishable pilgrim's garb and letter of commendation. He did not need health insurance as pilgrims' hospitals and monasteries would care for him. His embassy and protection abroad were the various orders founded to protect the pilgrim's interest in times of uncertainty.

A misericord from Great Malvern Priory showing acorn gathering. *Sarah Hopper*

Matthew Paris's drawing of two Knights Templar on one horse from his *Historia Anglorum*, mid-thirteenth century. This figure appears on the seal of the order and shows the first Templar Hugo de Payens and Godfrey de St Omer, Knights, whose poverty led them to share one horse. *MS 16:75r. The Masters and Fellows of Corpus Christi College, Cambridge*

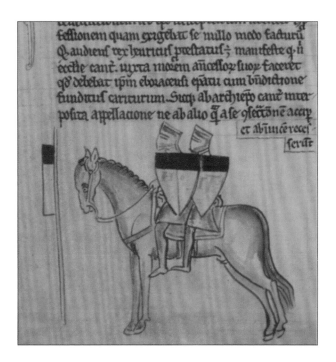

In Spain the Knights of St James attached to the shrine of Compostela were the familiar order. In the fifteenth century, King Ferdinand and Queen Isabella claimed the office of Master of the Knights of St James as their own. Perhaps of greater renown were the Knights of Malta, the conception of whose order was probably first mooted in Jerusalem in the eleventh century before the first crusade. Originally begun in a pilgrim's infirmary in Jerusalem, the order came to assume its military character as the need arose for pilgrims to be protected from Moslem attack. Their fame and activity permeated Christendom.

The Knights Templar were founded in the early twelfth century and were mostly famed for their protection of the pilgrim. Their seal portayed a knight coming to the aid of a pilgrim described as *pauper et peregrinus*. Theoderich in his thirteenth-century writings on the Holy Land attests to the role of the Knights Templar on the plains of the River Jordan.

> the Templars . . . practise . . . is to escort pilgrims who are going to the Jordan and to watch that they are not injured by the Saracens either in going or returning, or while passing the night there.[8]

Theoderich also testifies to their widespread occupancy of the Holy Land as a powerful, military presence.

> It is not easy for anyone to gain an idea of the power and wealth of the Templars – for they and the Hospitallers have taken possession of almost all the cities and villages . . . and have built castles everywhere and filled them with garrisons.[9]

With Pope Clement V's suppression of their cause in 1312, the remainder of their wealth was given to the Knights of Malta.

CHAPTER EIGHT

PILGRIM PATHS: THE JOURNEY

And by the happy, blissful way
More peaceful pilgrims I shall see.[1]

The routes to the popular pilgrimage sites of Europe and beyond soon became established paths. At the height of pilgrimage activity, most were also well equipped with hostels that were about a day's walk apart.[2] Other subsidiary routes existed if the pilgrim so chose, but for reasons of personal safety, orientation and the assurance of hostelry, it was advisable to keep to the most recognised paths, or those most frequented by other pilgrims.

One of the most well trodden trails in England was the road from Winchester to Canterbury, but there were also many others that served to create an accessible network of routes linking noteworthy shrines, for example from Old Sarum to Glastonbury, Ely to Walsingham, Hexham to Lindisfarne and Beverley Minster to York Minster. Along the routes a system of wayside crosses was used to show the pilgrim that he was taking the right road. These were positioned in such a way that they could be identified from a long way off, as well as at junctions and crossroads. Surviving examples occur at Binham on the Bromholme road to Walsingham (although the cross at the top no longer survives) and at Hockley cum Wilton on the Ely road to Walsingham. Today, walkers can still follow some of these routes. Others have chosen to do this further afield. Hilaire Belloc wrote of his journeys from Alsace to the Vatican as well as from Winchester to Canterbury in the early 1900s.

For those travelling through France on the way to Santiago de Compostela, there were four main overland routes to choose from. Each had a different starting point, the most westerly path beginning at Tours in the Loire Valley. This well provisioned route journeyed south through the Bordeaux region, offering the easiest terrain but the longest expedition. Many of those pilgrims arriving from England, having sailed from such ports as Dartmouth or Plymouth, would be able to join this route, perhaps making a detour to the grand cathedral of Notre Dame at Chartres on their way.

Herein, the thirteenth-century stained glass offered pilgrims a foretaste of the religious and political prestige of the land of their destination. A pair of windows in the choir relate Charlemagne's military campaign against the Arab Moors, depicting the two armies in full cavalry charge. Others are devoted to the life of Spain's patron, St James the Great, and his call to Charlemagne in a dream to return to

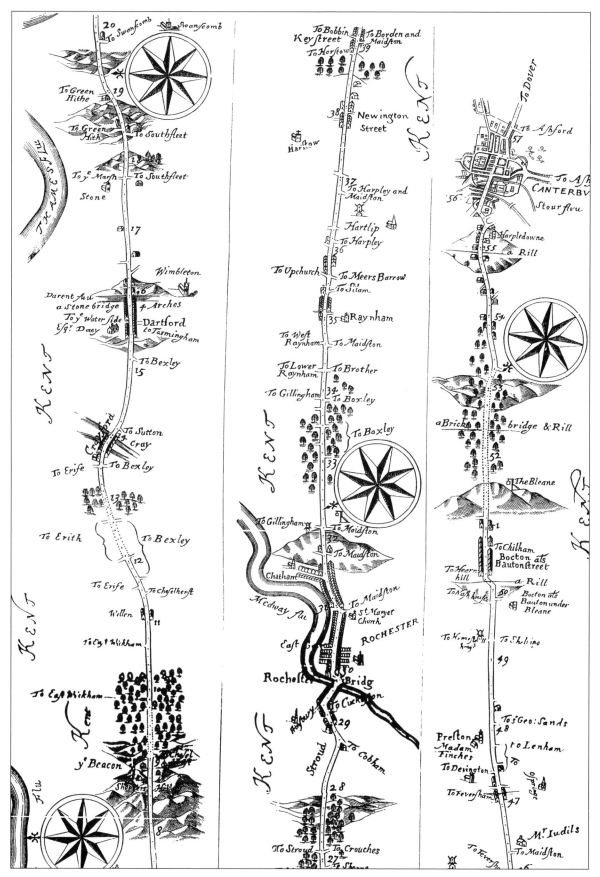

Ogilby's map of the road from London to Canterbury, *c.* 1675.

A map of English shrines.
Sarah Hopper

Spain and liberate it from the infidel. Chartres also exhibited a renowned statue of the Virgin and claimed possession of the tunic that she had worn on the day of the Anunciation, preserved there since 861.

Those others who set out from more easterly ports on England's south coast, such as Portsmouth, may have chosen to pass through Amiens, Paris and Orleans, as well as Chartres, before linking up with the Tours path. The call of prestigious relics and venerated sites sometimes required minor deviations on the pilgrim's path; for example, the cathedral at Amiens temporarily lured the English pilgrim east rather than south with its promise of a most holy pilgrim attraction, the head of John the Baptist.[3]

Between Orléans and Tours, those pilgrims journeying from Paris might have stopped at Vendôme where a curious, but no less revered relic was housed. The Abbey of the Trinity there was founded in 1032 by the Count of Anjou who subsequently supplied it with a collection of relics, which included a rock-crystal reliquary containing the holy tear shed by Christ on the occasion of Lazarus' revivification. As with relics of the holy blood, other French churches also claimed ownership of Christ's holy tears, but evidence suggests that the holy tear at Vendôme was the most celebrated.

As the convergence point for many pilgrims beginning their journey proper to Compostela, Tours offered its own archetypal pilgrim's church, that of St Martin. Indeed, in his pilgrim guide, Aimery Picaud draws a parallel between St Martin at Tours and the Cathedral of St James. Built on a large scale in the tenth and eleventh centuries, with wide aisles and transepts, apse and ambulatory, it was everything to which the medieval pilgrim was accustomed and that which he would encounter repeatedly along his way.

St Martin (d. AD 397) was held in great affection, and was one of the first early Christians to be venerated as a saint who had not been martyred. His miracle-working tomb led pilgrims to drink an elixir of water mixed with dust gathered from the tomb for its reported effects as a healing tonic. As a former bishop of Tours and the man who founded monasticism in France, St Martin's name raised the profile of Tours from an early stage. St Martin came to be honoured by many pilgrims who chose their route along the Via Turonensis beginning at Tours, and then crossed the

A stained-glass window in the choir of Chartres Cathedral showing Charlemagne fighting the Saracens. *John Crook*

A Pilgrim (right) crossing a bridge in Paris, while other men drag wine casks and unload coal from boats. Detail of a miniature from the *Life of St Denis*, 1317. *MS fr. 2091–2 flo. 1r. Bibliothèque Nationale, Paris/Bridgeman Art Library*

town's bridge over the Loire on their journey to Compostela. Saint-Jean-D'Angely provided another important staging post for the pilgrim on the Tours route, as its Benedictine monastery, like the cathedral at Amiens, claimed ownership of the head of St John the Baptist.

A second path commencing at Vézelay in Burgundy, the Via Viziliaci, took the pilgrim across the centre of France through Bourges and Limoges. Host to the Church of St Marie Madeleine, Vézelay was already a popular venue for pilgrims who wished to witness the holy relics of this revered saint. Originally said to have been carried back from the Holy Land by one of Vézelay's monks, the saint's remains were later claimed, as was so common a story, to have been stolen, in this case from Aix en Provence. These claims did not always influence the pilgrim's discretion, and such thefts were often accounted for as a *furtum sacrum*, or a theft excused for its pious motive. It was understood that the relics were merely being moved to a more suitable dwelling and that if they were not in agreement, their power would be sufficient to prevent it. In the case of Vézelay, though, mounting scandal about the theft did lead to a decline in the number of pilgrim visitors in the thirteenth century.

The basilica at Vézelay maintains an enchanting sense of mystery. Engulfed almost immediately by its covered porch with subdued lighting, the visitor is bound by the detailed carving of its tympanum, showing Christ in majesty with arms outstretched. The light of the church's interior drew the pilgrim within the nave and onward to its holy relics at the east end. Naturally, the cogent ambience of this passage into the church led pilgrims to see it as an allegorical spiritual journey, from the temporal to the divine.

East of Limoges, a church dedicated to St Leonard offered a curious sight for pilgrims. As well as being the patron of pregnant women, St Leonard was also champion of the incarcerated. The beams of the church were hung with all manner of irons, foot clamps, chains and stocks left by those freed prisoners as symbols of their liberation and thanks for the intercession of the saint on their behalf. Parodies with the incarceration of St Peter might also have been in mind when venerating this particular saint. The Vézelay path charted a route down through the Limoges valley, through the Dordogne to join with the Tours and Le Puy routes at Ostabat.

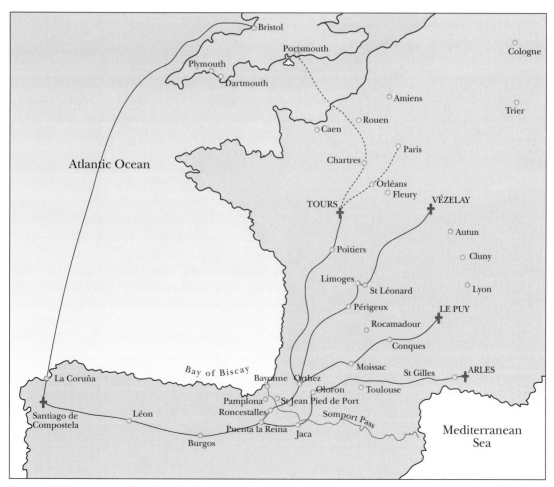

A map of the routes to Santiago de Compostela in northern Spain. *Sarah Hopper*

From the third starting point at Le Puy, the pilgrim was set on the Via Podiensis that would pass though Conques and Moissac. At Le Puy stood the Hospital of Saint Mary dedicated to Our Lady of Le Puy. In the abbey church at Conques, the pilgrim could see the spectacular reliquary of the early Gallic martyr, Saint Faith. A wooden statue enveloped in gold and silver sheets, the figure is shown seated on a throne and encrusted with jewels and gems. Another example of a *furtum sacrum*, the relics it contained were stolen from the church at Agen by one of St Foy's monks in the ninth century.

One of the singular features of the church at Conques is its captivating Romanesque stone carving, particularly in the porch and tympanum. In an austere reminder of the pious pilgrim's motives for pilgrimage, the harrowing scenes of the Last Judgement are explicitly laid out. Demons spear and plague the damned who endure all manner of torturous, violent fates, while new conscripts are thrown into the open jaws of hell to join them. On the left half of the tympanum, the saints and the elect are gathered in paradise, hosted in the centre by Christ, seated in serene majesty. The juxtaposition of hell and paradise must have served as a valuable reminder to the pilgrim of what was at stake.

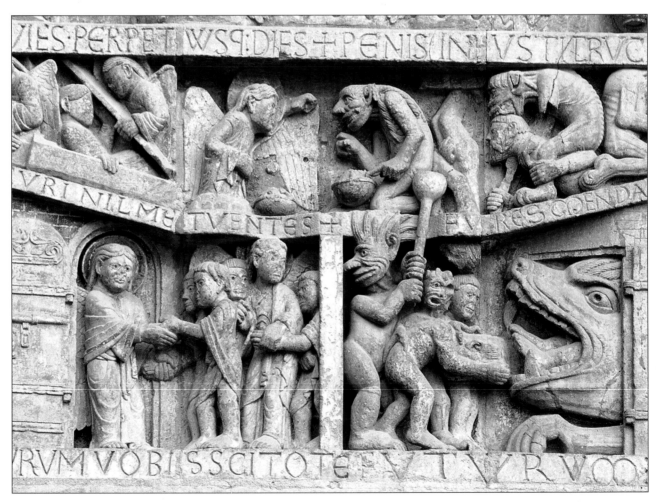

The tympanum of the church at Conques. *John Crook*

Rocamadour, to the north west of Conques, was also popular with pilgrims; it was visited by Simon de Montfort and Henry II among others. Requiring a rather rocky detour, the shrine was found on a cliff reached by flights of steps. The peak of Rocamadour's fame coincided with the year of Becket's martyrdom in 1170 when England's king, Henry II chose to make a pilgrimage here. Prior to his visit, many miracles had been attributed to the grace of Our Lady of Rocamadour.

Its shrine, dedicated to the Virgin Mary, was scattered with tufts and locks of hair. While an awe-inspiring sight, the significance of this gesture by pilgrims would have been understood. The most popular legend relating to the shrine speaks of a woman, afflicted with blindness as a result of her lascivious life style. Her sight was restored when she came to Rocamadour and offered up her prayers to the Virgin. Before the woman could enter the sanctuary though, she was ordered by the priest to cut off her long hair in honour of the Virgin. As with the tresses of many women before, her hair was cut, carried into the church and displayed as a reminder to all women saved from personal vanity by the Virgin's grace. However, on leaving the sanctuary the woman began to lament her decision. In an instant, her hair was returned to her head, and blindness to her eyes.

One of Edward II's yeomen, Gerald Donum, went on pilgrimage to the Church of St Mary at Rocamadour. This was in fulfillment of a vow he had made at a moment when his life was in danger at sea. He also pledged to maintain his beard until he reached Rocamadour where he would cut it and leave it at the church as a symbol of his salvation at the hands of the Virgin.[4]

The fourth route, beginning at Arles, near the mouth of the Rhône, assumed a westward path to Santiago, passing through Toulouse. This was the best route for pilgrims who had travelled south from Aachen, Cologne and Trier in Germany. Cologne attracted many pilgrims of its own, on account of its shrine to the Three Kings, the namesake of many a pilgrim's refuge on the road to Compostela. In 1125, William of Malmesbury, who also wrote a life of Saint Wulfstan, had described Cologne as Germany's metropolis with its own legion of esteemed saints. It was here that the relics of the Magi, or the Three Kings, were said to be laid to rest, having been transferred from Milan in 1162. Also venerated at Cologne was St Ursula, whose uncovered remains could also be seen there. In 1394 Cologne also offered pilgrims plenary indulgence, as granted by Pope Boniface IX.

The relics of the Three Kings were housed in a spectacular gold shrine begun by the highly skilled goldsmith Nicholas of Verdun in 1191. It depicts the Magi presenting their offerings to the baby Christ at a Romanesque church. This scene was also adopted for pilgrim badges from the Three Kings Shrine at Cologne.

An early pause on the Arles route was found at the Church of St Gilles du Gard in the Bouches du Rhône. The intriguing roots of St Gilles' sainthood are found in the legend of his life as a young Athenian hermit in Arles, who had rejected urban life for the forest. When he was killed by huntsmen, a monastery was constructed in his honour under the Visigoth king and his complete remains were preserved as relics there.

As with the legend of St James, this enchanting tradition fired the imagination of pilgrims. The relics of St Gilles also performed wondrous miracles, reportedly substantiated as the remains survived in their entirety. Carvings at the church offered the familiar Christological scenes of the pilgrim tour, as well as a particularly poignant rendering of the Kiss of Judas.

The capital of a pillar showing the sleep of the Magi, twelfth century, Cathedral of St Lazare, Autun, France.
Giraudon/Bridgeman Art Library

About halfway along the Arles route, before crossing the Pyrenees at the Somport Pass, was the Church of Saint Sernin, at Toulouse, which celebrated another martyred saint. South of the Pyrenees, the Arles route conjoined with the other three at Puente La Reina, or the Queen's Bridge. Before the Pyrenees, the Tours, Vézelay and Le Puy routes all intersected near Ostabat. Aimery Picaud's guide to the routes to Compostela tells us that pilgrims had to endure the hardships of flies and marshy terrain on this stretch of the Atlantic coast, before crossing into Spain. Pilgrim traffic also increased. The guide also noted the difficulties involved in crossing the two rivers in the foot hills of the Pyrenees, in France, near the village of St Jean de Sorder (Sorde l'Abbaye). It was impossible for pilgrims to cross these on foot, and therefore enterprising businessmen had a thriving trade ferrying pilgrims across in their less than sturdy boats. The guide cursed the shrewd perfidy of these ferrymen who charged four times as much for horses as for pilgrims, and sometimes deliberately overloaded the boat so that many pilgrims drowned and their belongings could be stolen by the ferrymen.[5] Today, many pilgrims begin from St Jean Pied de Port, crossing the Pyrenees on the first day, and then descending into Roncesvalles in Spain, a popular starting point for native pilgrims.

Crossing the Pyrenees could be avoided if pilgrims travelled by boat from one of England's southern ports to the north-west coast of Spain. It was also possible to travel by sea to the west coast of France and join the Tours route about a third of the way along and continue the journey over land and the Pyrenees. Whichever path was chosen, the journey offered a host of varying terrain and scenery, from winding mountain tracks to open countryside.

At San Salvador de Ibañeta in the vicinity of Roncevalles, a chapel was founded in 1071 marking the pilgrim's official entry into the land of St James. On the western road to Galicia, many offered up their prayers to the apostle saint here. Also commemorated is the folk hero, Roland, who having joined Charlemagne in the fierce wars against the Moors, met his untimely end at Roncesvalles. Picaud tells us of the many crosses that were planted by pilgrims here at the top of the Cisa Pass, just as Charlemagne had done at the start of his Spanish campaign.

From Puente La Reina the independent routes continued as one path through Burgos, Léon and on to Compostela. Built in the eleventh century to assist the pilgrim in crossing the River Arga, the distinctive six-arched bridge at Puente La Reina is still used by pilgrims today. In 1142 the Knights Templar settled in the town, at the request of García VI, to protect the interests of the pilgrim.

At the foot of the Cantabrian mountains at Triacastela, the pilgrim picked himself a piece of limestone which he would take with him to be calcined en route and then offered as lime for the fabric of St James's Cathedral. Only a few days distance from Compostela, the pilgrim would prepare himself for entry into the holy city by bathing in the river at Lavamentula. Picaud marks this practice as an act of reverence to the apostle saint, but for many it also meant losing their clothes to thieves! From here the pilgrim could also climb the *mons gaudii* to witness the focus of his pilgrimage, seemingly only an arm's length away – the city of Compostela.

Most pilgrims journeying to Rome came along the Via Francigena, an important route that led tradesmen, merchants, travelling ecclesiastics and pilgrims from north-western Europe to Rome. The usual method of crossing the Alps was by the Mont Cenis or the Mont Joux further north (Mons Iovis, later called the Great St Bernard). From the summit of Mont Cenis, the pilgrim could stay at an abbey dedicated to St Peter and a ninth-century hospice before his descent into northern Italy. The Great and Little St Bernard Pass were named in honour and memory of the charitable work of Bernard of Aosta in the Alpine region. Crossing of the Alps in itself could be an arduous journey, as the twelfth-century letter from a Master John at the Great St Bernard Pass indicates.

> Forgive my not writing, I have been on the Mons Jovis [Great St Bernard Pass] ... I put my hand in my scrip to scratch out a word or two to your sincerity; behold I found my ink bottle filled with a dry mass of ice. My fingers refused to write; my beard was stiff with frost, and my breath congealed in a long icicle. I could not write.[6]

The first literary mention of the route that the Via Francigena followed is in the diary of Archbishop Sigeric of Canterbury from 993. His diary entries record his journey back to Canterbury, having visited Rome, and detail the stops that he made on the way. These included Siena, San Gimignano and Lucca, all of cultural interest to the visitor, and even now exquisitely reminiscent of medieval Italy. Crossing the Apennines via the Mons Bardonis Pass rather than the Cisa Pass, Sigeric proceeded

A thirteenth-century view of pilgrims travelling by ship, Basilica of San Francesco, Mallorca, Spain. *Bridgeman Art Library*

north through Piacenza and Vercelli, traversing the Alps by Aosta and the Great
St Bernard Pass.

For the journey towards Rome, the Via Francigena crossed four distinctive,
topographical areas of Italy. Entering the region of Tuscany at the Cisa Pass in the
Apennines, it followed the valley of the Magra River down to Sarzana where the Via
Francigena intersected with another Roman road, the Aurelia. Hugging the Apuane
mountains, the route continues to Lucca along open, undulating terrain to
Altopascio, an important centre for pilgrims that was well provided with hostelry
and so on. Continuing though open territory towards Fucecchio and Siena, the
pilgrim passed through many towns en route, including Castelfiorentino and
Poggibonsi. From Siena, the route continued south to Abbadia San Salvatore with its
eighth-century abbey. This led through hilly countryside, passing by the sulphur
springs of Bagno Vignoni, revered for the water's curative properties.

While for many pilgrims the journey to Rome was initiated with crossing France,
others used a route through Germany. Such a course was taken by the chronicler
Adam of Usk on his journey to Rome in 1402. Embarking at Billingsgate on
19 February, he landed at Brabant and then wended his way through Holland,
Germany, Switzerland and down the leg of Italy. He notes how he was careful to
avoid certain places in Italy, such as Bologna and Florence, on account of threats of
siege by the Duke of Milan. With stops at all the noted hostels lasting about two days

each, Adam arrived in Rome on the 5 April. His journey also assumed an ethereal sense with the presence of a comet that was visible during March and April of that year.

While astronomy had its own place in medieval society as one of the strands of learning, many superstitions were attached to their advent. In this instance, Adam states that the comet spread terror among those who witnessed it. He understood it as a premonition of the death of the Duke of Milan who, he informs us, 'did in fact die soon after this'.[7]

England was also subject to a passing comet in the eleventh century, as depicted on the Bayeux Tapestry. A similarly morbid interpretation was held that it not only foreshadowed the death of England's king, Edward the Confessor, but was a bad portent for the future of Harold. In his writings on the history of the English church and people, Bede notes that in the year AD 664, an outbreak of plague was predetermined by an eclipse.[8]

Many pilgrims who visited Rome would then travel overland en route to the Holy Land. They would arrive at Venice, the 'gateway to the East', to pick up a galley that would take them the rest of the way to Jaffa. This sometimes meant waiting at Venice for weeks, even months, until one became available and was ready to sail. While in Venice though, pilgrims could spend their time wisely by purchasing the rest of the provisions and bedding that they would require for the uncertain voyage ahead. On the return trip, they could sell such items back to the same vendor at a discount. William Wey, in his *Itineraries to Jerusalem*, suggests that pilgrims should

get a feather bed, matress, 2 pillows, 2 pairs of sheets, a quilt.[9]

Pilgrims would be able to visit the churches of Venice's patron saints, Raphael, Michael, Christopher and Martha, who were all appropriately associated with safe travel. Faber also described visiting the churches of SS John and Paul, where he drank the water of St Peter, and was blessed with the curative powers of the saints' relics. He explains the extended use of this holy water by mariners who put a drop of it into their drinking water on board ship to prevent stagnation. Pilgrims could also visit St Mark's Square, St Mark's Church and admire the Doges' Palace. From here, two galleys had been arranged to take pilgrims to the Holy Land, and two nobles had been entrusted with their care.

Perhaps the most lucid desciption of securing passage from Venice to the port of Jaffa is in Faber's account. He described the two pilgrim ships offered to him, that of Master Augustine Contanini, with whom he had travelled on his first trip to the Holy Land, and the second belonging to Master Peter de Lando. Persuasive and resourceful, both spread out wine and delicacies on their ship's poops in order to win the custom of Faber and his companions. This time, Faber chose the boat of de Lando, not out of fairness, having declined his offer of passage three years before, but because it was a triple instead of double-banked galley.

The journey from Venice took the pilgrims across the long stretch of the Mediterranean Sea to Jaffa. This journey could include stops at any of the Mediterranean islands with their own growing repertoire of venerated sites and native saints. Saewulf's itinerary mentions stops at the islands of Corfu, Cephalonia, Crete and Samos, to name but four. For some, on completion of their tour of the Holy Land's sites, a journey by boat from Jaffa to Cyprus was possible, or for the more

The cave of Agios Gerasimos, patron saint of Cephalonia. *Ben Hopper*

adventurous, an overland journey from Jerusalem to Cairo crossing the Sinai Desert.

Such journeys by land and sea were sometimes recorded and their details related among other pilgrims for the wisdom and experience they offered. At the beginning of his own pilgrimage accounts, Brother Belard of Ascoli plainly states that he has recorded all the things he saw so that his writings may be of use to others.

The earliest of such guidebooks were often known as *itineraria*, quite simply a suggested itinerary of sites worthy of visit. In the case of Rome, the earliest of these were probably based on Roman military maps. Others offered advice based on personal experience, such as the twelfth-century *Book of Roger* compiled from the stories of pilgrims and travelling merchants. The first printed guidebook in English was the *Informacion for Pylgrymes Unto the Holy Land* compiled by the protégé of William Caxton, Wynken de Worde, using the writings and information of an experienced medieval traveller, William Wey.

Some guides, such as the *Liber Sancti Jacobi* written in the twelfth century, advised on the different races of people that would be encountered en route to Compostela. The writer is relentless in his criticism of various peoples, particularly in his venomous depiction of the Basques, whom he describes as perfidious, disloyal, savage and impious. He notes also that the people of Navarre are badly dressed and adopt poor table manners, eating like gluttonous pigs and sounding like barking dogs when they speak. Worse still, it is stated that they fornicate with beasts![10]

Such guidebooks often warned fellow pilgrims and travellers of known dangers and advised of the best and safest routes to take. For example, the *Veneranda Dies*, within the *Liber Sancti Jacobi*, draws attention to a particular stretch of road that led to Compostela through France and the Pyrenees that had become a black spot, harbouring an organised network of thieves. He also cites Lucca, Tours, Rome, Le Puy and others as centres for duplicity and fraud.

Some of the laws that were enforced in efforts to ensure greater protection of the pilgrim give us a better idea of the type of dangers they were up against. The first Lateran Council in 1123 threatened excommunication to all those that stole from pilgrims. During the reign of Richard I (1189–99), a law was enacted to protect pilgrims travelling to the Holy Land.

> He who kills a man on shipboard shall be bound to the dead body and thrown into the sea. He who shall draw his knife to strike another, or who shall have drawn blood from him, to lose his hand; if he shall only have struck with the palm of his hand without drawing blood, he shall be thrice ducked in the sea.[11]

In 1229, the King of Spain, Alfonso IX declared that all pilgrims of God and St James should be free from any such mistreatment or indignity throughout his kingdom.

Many pilgrim accounts, such as the famous Paston letters, surviving correspondence of a fifteenth-century, Norfolk family, recount the abduction and attack of pilgrims. Margery Kempe speaks of two English pilgrims returning to England from Rome who had been robbed along with a friar in their party. As a result, they were left with barely enough money to get themselves home.[12]

Brother Felix Faber offers his own account of a group of English pilgrims that he first encountered in the Holy Land. He had chosen not to pursue company with them as they did not speak his own German or Latin. Nonetheless, he is later reunited with them in Trent, Germany. They had been beaten, wounded and robbed in a nearby wood. The perpetrators had even gone to the trouble of asking their victims to strip, so that they could investigate for any money sewn into their clothes.

Another preventative measure against pilgrim attack was the clear marking of routes so that they should not become disorientated and vulnerable. Equally, it made sense to the benefactors of important sites to assist in making the pilgrims journey and visit as agreeable and accessible as possible.

In Rome, Pope Damascus (302–84) organised a system of signposting in the catacombs at Rome that took the form of verse inscriptions. It is thought that these helped pilgrims until the eighth century. Pope Symmachus (d. 514) also worked to ensure the welfare of the pilgrim and later, in the seventh century, Pope Honorius I (625–38) wrote his *notitia ecclesiarum urbis Romae* that detailed a perimeter tour of Rome enabling the pilgrim to visit the notable churches and burial sites en route. Outside of Rome Stephen of Hungary (975–1038) ordered routes to be set down for pilgrims to Jerusalem. Various kings and queens of Spain also played their part in assisting the pilgrim cause.

Even working from surviving accounts that note date of departure and return, it remains difficult to gain a definitive answer as to how long such journeys took the pilgrim by land and sea. This is partly because the pilgrim's itinerary would include several side trips to other shrines, sometimes spontaneous, as well as unforseen periods of sickness and recovery and inevitable delays. This latter problem is related by Margery Kempe. She describes how on arrival at the port of Bristol she waited for her passage for six weeks. Her arrival had been untimely as it coincided with Henry V's requisitioning of ships for his expedition to France in 1417.[13]

The same problem was encountered by Brother Faber who waited at Venice for many days before his galley was fitted for sea. As a result of the frustrations and weariness that this caused, on his second journey to the Holy Land, Faber drew up a contract that stipulated that the captain should be ready to leave in fourteen days and no longer, and that no unnecessary pit stops should be made but for food.[14] However, on arrival at Jaffa, Faber and his companions were forced to wait on board for seven days before their obligatory guides arrived. They then made a further stop at the town of Ramleh where they were made to lodge for some days before proceeding to Jerusalem.[15]

William Wey recorded his experiences of his two journeys to the Holy Land in 1458 and in 1462. It is noted that his first journey took thirty-nine weeks and of that time, thirteen days were spent in the Holy Land potentially leaving another thirty-seven weeks worth of travelling time, although some of this may have been consumed by visits to further places of interest en route. In the twelfth century, Saewulf, having chosen a less direct route across the Mediterranean to Jaffa, stopping at many of its islands en route, states that this part of his journey alone took thirteen weeks. In 1139, Reynold of Evesham took forty-nine days to travel from Canterbury to Rome, while in 1188, two papal mandates, travelling the journey in reverse from Rome to Canterbury, made the journey in twenty-nine and twenty-five days respectively. It seems likely that they were forced to practice stricter timekeeping as they were on a papal mission.

Perhaps sea travel presented the most delays, concerns and dangers for the pilgrim. The most common types of ship were double or triple-banked galleys. The owners and captains of such ships were granted licences authorising them to carry pilgrims to their destination. These were often drawn up in Latin, the language of official and government documents, naming the ship, its owner and captain and stating the points of embarkation and destination. These also included the specific number of pilgrims to be carried by the said ship (usually between thirty and a hundred) and the agreement that pilgrims would also be given return passage. Many of these licences have survived from the fourteenth century, and it is from these that the most accurate conclusion can be drawn as to the numbers of pilgrims travelling to sites such as Santiago de Compostela.[16]

Various ports in England operated as starting points for such journeys, having been granted licences to carry pilgrims. Richard II was particularly scrupulous in controlling of the exportation of pilgrims overseas. All such pilgrims were obliged to carry passports granting them the leave of their king to undertake their sea voyage. These could be obtained from selective ports, as appointed by the king, including Dover, Plymouth, Weymouth and London. Later in the fourteenth century, the king restricted the pilgrim's choice of port to Dover and Plymouth. These regulations coincided with a period of greater movement of people in and out of England and a growing trend for a trade in smuggling.

The weather at sea was another major peril for the pilgrim, and it was during such hazardous instances that vows for further pilgrimages were made, if only their lives would be spared. Saewulf relates how he arrived at Jaffa just in time before a raging storm blew up. It spared only seven of the thirty large ships in the port which were laiden with merchandise and pilgrims. Another document related the effects of being caught up in such a storm on board ship.

Healthy men become weak during a storm, and sick men grow weaker still.[17]

There is much evidence to suggest that many pilgrims were ill-accustomed to sea journeys and consequently fell ill en route. Descriptions of the effects of storms at sea are fairly common in surviving pilgrim accounts. Faber offers perhaps the most lucid and dramatic accounts of the hardships at sea. He describes how in a storm, he and his companions either raced to cling to the pillars in the middle of the cabin, or else crouched on the floor as fierce winds dashed their main sail. An eruption of prayers, confessions and the making of vows usually ensued. The power of the sea was not to be underestimated. It is the wise that fear the sea's strength, while fools hold it cheap.

[The sea] strikes terror into the soul; it causes headache, it provokes vomiting and nausea; it destroys appetite for food and drink; it acts as an alterative on the human body; it excites the passions and produces many strange vices; it causes extreme and deadly perils, and often brings men to a most cruel death.[18]

In Faber's account, the problem of sea sickness among the pilgrims also gave rise to another practical problem, whether the Eucharist should be performed on board ship. Faber cites fifteen reasons against it, including the risk of a storm rising just after the ceremony and the pilgrim vomiting forth the sacrament![19]

Equally, conditions on board could be squalid and unhygienic, with everyone packed into one confined space. Any germs were quickly shared by all. Pilgrims would be assigned berths and cots in the galley of the ship, and would be required to pack away their bedding each morning and re-lay it at night in order to keep the galley clear. There is much to suggest that pilgrims were not made to feel altogether welcome on such journeys. One tale relates how on returning to ship, the pilgrims found that their cabins had been filled with planks of wood.[20]

In his contract, drawn up for the captain of one such ship, Faber's experience on a previous pilgrimage to the Holy Land had led him to specify certain ground rules. Among these were that pilgrims' berths should not be interfered with, that if any of the pilgrims should die, their belongings should not be meddled with, and also that pilgrims should be protected from molestation by the ship's slaves. Wey had advised the purchase of a chest complete with padlock to carry on to the ship. Faber also states that pilgrims should be given proper burial on the nearest land. Surely disconcerting for Faber and his companions was seeing a dead body brought to shore by the waves.

William Wey offers practical advice for pilgrims on embarkation: 'And chose you a place in the sayd galey in the overmost stage, for in the lowest under it is ryght evyll and smouldryng hote and stynkynge.'[21] He advises that a pilgrim should choose a cabin: '. . . as nyghe the myddes of the shippe as ye may, for there is leest rollynge or tomblinge to kepe your brayne and stomache in tempre. And in the same chambre to kepe your thynges in saufgarde. And bye you at Venyse a padlocke to hange on the doore when ye shall pass in to the londe.'[22] Pilgrims would bring with them all

Three travellers aboard ship, from the west face of the twelfth-century Tournai marble font in Winchester Cathedral. *John Crook*

the practical items that they required for the journey, these normally being purchased in Venice before embarkation, such as woollen blankets, sheets, mats, pillows, cushions and mattresses (stuffed with straw or animal hair).

One suspects that when night fell, pilgrims felt the discomforts of galley conditions at their worst. Several sources mention problems such as the close proximity of other pilgrims – limiting movement in the night. The loud snores of other pilgrims and moans of the sick pervaded the squalid air, thick with foul odours. Mice and rats run amok, helping themselves to the pilgrim's private larders and gnawing at their bedding and clothes. Mosquitoes, fleas and lice were rife in the claustrophobic heat. According to Faber, unless the pilgrim spent a good portion of his time hunting down the lice and vermin, he would enjoy very little in the way of sleep.

Margery Kempe's own experience reveals how pilgrims were inevitably affected by such conditions. Coming into the company of a group of poorer pilgrims who were surviving their journey on handouts and begging, Kempe regularly witnessed them undressing in order to pick themselves for vermin: 'Through mixing with them, she caught some of their vermin and was dreadfully bitten and stung both day and night, until God sent her other companions.'[23]

The food on board ship presented another health hazard. While Faber's contract stated that pilgrims should be given two meals of food and drink a day, food aboard ship was wont to turn stale at alarming speed. As a result, worm-infested food, off meat and putrid water had to be endured. Worse still was the shortage or complete lack of food when stops for supplies were rendered impossible by war, weather or plague. This was the experience of Faber and his companions who endured their return journey from Jaffa without food or water. He poignantly states how having lived through this experience, it is beyond him that people should suffer such angst over a forty-day fast for Lent. Even on land, foreign food and climate could pose health risks for the pilgrim. Perhaps the most forthright observation on this comes from the author of the twelfth century *Guide du Pelerin* (possibly by the same author as the *Liber Sancti Jacobi*), who advises simply that all fish, beef and pork throughout Spain and Galicia made foreigners ill.[24]

Of all the guides, perhaps the recorded journeys of the fifteenth-century Eton fellow, William Wey (1408–76), to Compostela and twice to the Holy Land, offer the most candid advice for pilgrims. Wey's verse and prose were heavily drawn upon by Wynkyn de Worde in order to compile his *Information for Pilgrims Unto the Holy Land*.

> beware of fruytes that ye ete none for no thynge. As melons and suche colde fruytes, for they be not accordynge to our complexyon & they gendre a blody fluxe [diarrhoea]. And yf ony enghysshe man catche there that syknesse, it is a grete merueylle but yt he deye therof.[25]

He also suggests packing a good supply of laxatives and other medicines.

Many pilgrims also suffered as a result of the exhausting heat in the Holy Land. Faber relates how he and his companions returned so weakened and ill that their ship took the appearance of a hospital of sick invalids. Two of his companions died as a result, and on arrival at Venice, Faber was forced to stay in the care of doctors for another two weeks, unable to walk.

Perhaps the most alarming of dangers was the threat of plague. Faber tells how his ship taking the usual route from Venice to Jaffa came into port on the

Dalmatian coast (modern-day Dubrovnik) to discover it had been overcome with plague. Some instances of plague were indeed outbreaks of the Bubonic Plague, which first struck England in 1348 and returned several times until the end of the seventeenth century. The word 'plague' or 'pestilence' though was generally used to apply to any of the many epidemics that affected medieval society, often as a result of squalid, unhygienic living conditions. Not surprisingly, the towns were often worst affected.

The Paston letters offer an interesting insight into the fear associated with the uncontrollable spread of disease. On 6 November 1479 John Paston III wrote to his elder brother of how the disease had spread to Norwich affecting every house in the city with sickness and death, so that his wife would not go out of doors.[26] It is interesting to note from another of the Paston letters that there was, by this stage, an apparent awareness of the association between dirt and disease. Sir John Paston II wrote to his mother on 29 October 1479 after two weeks in London, saying that he had found his room and belongings to be dirty, which greatly concerned him with his 'fear of the sickness'.[27]

As Rome's coffers abounded in light of the increasing number of pilgrims, it also encountered severe overcrowding, which brought disease. Spain also fell victim to plague as is movingly described in a pilgrim's hymn:

> Vous qui allez a Sainct Iacques,
> Je vous prie humblement
> Que n'ayez point de haste:
> Allez tout bellement,
> Has! Ques les pauvres malades
> Sont en grand désconfort!
> Car Maints hommes et femmes
> Par les chemins sont morts.[28]

A less grave danger for pilgrims involved disembarking the ship on arrival in a port, although Faber considers it worthy of note. He describes the pilgrim's dangerous leap from the galley into a boat, one that resulted in occasional misjudgement.

Although not life-threatening, another significant issue that is noted in the writings of some pilgrims was that of problem companions, sometimes as criminal and untrustworthy as they were deeply irritating. Faber witnesses the personality clashes that occurred between fellow travellers with the comment: 'for if a man has a comrade with whom he cannot agree, woe betide them both during their pilgrimage'.[29]

He touches on the issue of class distinction. He related how two proud nobles on their way to receive their honorary knighthoods refused to sail in the same ship as an elderly woman already aboard. Pilgrimage threw people from all walks of life together in what could become a melting pot of intolerance and class tension. On a brighter note, we are reminded also that such hardship and intimacy also served to forge friendships and bonds on board. Parting company afterwards was sometimes a sorrowful occasion.[30]

Perhaps the best examples of problem companions are in the dictated writings of Margery Kempe. As a lone female traveller, she speaks of her difficulties with fellow pilgrims who steal from her, rebuke and abandon her and show a general lack of charity where she is concerned. 'Also this company, which had excluded the said creature from their table so that she should no longer eat amongst them, arranged a ship for themselves to sail in.'[31] Much of the reason for the isolation that Margery Kempe endures concerns her routine unrestrained outbursts of pious emotion. These label her as annoying to others who become intolerant of her.

> And as soon as it was perceived that she was going to cry, she would hold it in as much as she could, so that people would not hear it and get annoyed. For some said it was an illness; some said she had drunk too much wine; some cursed her; some wished she was in the harbour; some wished she was on the sea in a bottomless boat; and so each man as he thought.[32]

As a female pilgrim Kempe was concerned about issues of personal safety. She speaks of 'indecent looks' and fears for her chastity in the company of male pilgrims.[33] On one occasion, at hostelry on her way to Aachen and deserted by the rest of her company, Kempe requests the lady of the house to let her have some of the maids sleep in her bed with her for security. Nevertheless, she is unable to sleep in fear of being violated. She repeated this practice many times. 'She dared trust no man; whether she had reason or not, she was always afraid. She scarcely dared sleep any night.'[34]

Pietro Azario reflected

> O how dangerous it is to lead attractive, nay beautiful young women (in whom levity and lust are inherent) into foreign parts . . . particularly inexperienced wives. . . . Bernadino da Polenta, lord of the cities of Ravenna and Cervia . . . debauched many young and noble women . . . who were on their way to Rome in the last jubilee year, 1350.[35]

Other impediments to female pilgrims included their prohibited entry to certain places, such as the confines of a monastery. This was the case when women arrived to witness the relics of St Benoît at Fleury. While the men in the group were allowed into the monastery, the women were left standing at the gates. After much wrangling and pleading, a pavilion was erected outside the gates where the relics were temporarily displayed for the women.[36] A similar situation occurred at Pontigny, where in order to satisfy the women's pious devotion, the arm of the saint was brought outside for them to witness. On this occasion though, it was felt that God had become displeased by the dismemberment of the saint's remains, and from here on the relics refused to perform miracles publicly.

While monks could seek permission to undertake pilgrimage, it was made more difficult for nuns. Although some managed to gain special dispensation, for example the Abbess of Minster, in Thanet, Kent, who had first sought the counsel of the Pope, there was still a strong sense of scepticism and opposition to the idea from as early as the fourth century. This resistance stemmed partly from the belief that the duties of the cloistered nun were within the convent, and her sufferings therein would shorten her period in purgatory. In essence, she did not need to go on a pilgrimage to commend herself to God, as she had already vowed herself to his service.

There was an element of sexism towards women who undertook pilgrimage. There is much evidence that suggests that the constitution of the female was not

The Cathedral at Santiago de Compostela, showing the Shrine of St James. *John Crook*

robust enough to endure such a journey. In the Holy Land, Margery Kempe struggled up the Mount of Temptation, thirsty and tired. Her male companions show her no sympathy and she is eventually rescued by a handsome and somewhat more chivalrous Saracen who carries her to the top. Admittedly, Margery Kempe later confesses to having regular difficulty in keeping up with her male companions and enduring as long a day's walking as they are able. Her subsequent confession that she is normally unaccustomed to walking and is also about sixty years old earn her greater merit for her zeal and enthusiasm, whatever her sex.[37] In another insight, Jerome's letter to Eustochium comments how Paula, another female pilgrim to Jerusalem, exhibited 'a zeal and courage unbelievable in a woman, she forgot her sex and her physical weakness.'[38]

The lascivious conduct of some female pilgrims was held up to scrutiny by those who spoke out against the abuses of pilgrimage. Both female tavern workers and pilgrims were targeted for their promiscuous behaviour, as it was unbefitting of the pious meaning of pilgrimage. Needless to say, misconduct and impropriety among pilgrims went across the board, while the behaviour of female pilgrims attracted more reproach.

CHAPTER NINE

BY THE WAYSIDE: CATERING FOR THE PILGRIM

They bare with them no manner of thing
That was worth a farthing
Goods, gold nor possessions;
But meekly they asked their meat
Where that they might it get
For Saint Charity.[1]

As far as is known, the earliest lodgings in existence in the eighth and ninth centuries for the sheltering of the weary and the traveller were the *xenodochium* of monastic and Church provision. In the same way that giving alms to the poor was advocated as an act of pious charity, monasteries and the faithful were encouraged by the Church to accommodate the weary pilgrim within their precincts. Monasteries were even advised to set aside a proportion of their revenue in order to supply such hospitality. To receive or assist a pilgrim was to share in the merit and virtue of his journey. The notion of honouring Christ in every stranger also asserted by Jesus himself to his disciples:

> Whoever welcomes you welcomes me; and whoever welcomes me welcomes the one who sent me. Whoever welcomes God's messenger because he is God's messenger, will share in his reward. . . . You can be sure that whoever gives even a drink of cold water to one of the least of these my followers because he is my follower, will certainly receive a reward.[2]

Monastic houses offered a kind of open house to all types and classes of pilgrim, including the poor and foreigners. Monks and clergy were given special consideration. Guests would be fed and given a blessing before they set off again, so that they were spiritually as well as physically rejuvenated by their stay. For those pilgrims requiring medical attention, monasteries also had their own infirmaries within the grounds. The Cluniac monasteries are perhaps the best known for their hospitality to the pilgrim.

Pilgrims fortunate enough to find lodgings within the Guesten Hall of Christ Church Priory, Canterbury, were assured of hospitality as a result of the statutes of

The ruins outside Winchester Cathedral. *Sarah Hopper*

Archbishop Winchelsea. These dictated that pilgrim guests should be fed daily with bread and meat. Also, if any should die there, whatever his rank or nationality, he should receive the privilege of burial within the cathedral grounds. Royal visitors to Canterbury were housed in Saint Augustine's Abbey.

Those monastic houses in the vicinity of the larger, more famous shrines were more likely to receive wealthier pilgrims and those of noble background. Moreover, such guests would be in a position to pay for such charity, while monasteries were obliged to shelter the poor for free. So it was that in these instances, the wealthy and the nobility were given preferential treatment. Monastic houses also expressed a material interest in encouraging guests to make donations of money to their institution, many offering their own display of holy relics. In exchange, the donor would receive the much sought-after indulgences which for many were one of the main stimuli for pilgrimage.

Naturally, some monastic hostels offered better service to their guests than others and evidence supplied by medieval chroniclers highlights the distinctions between them. Abbot Agelwy of Evesham Abbey was particularly benevolent in his provision of shelter for the pilgrim and made it a ritual to wash the feet of all who entered.

The Pilgrim's Hall, Winchester Cathedral. *John Crook*

A religious allegory with Christ's washing of his disciples' feet is apparent here. In fact, this was a duty required of such hosts by the Church, but one that seems readily disregarded.

As the numbers of pilgrims increased many monasteries struggled to accommodate them; so special guest halls were often erected. This was the case at Worcester Cathedral for example where the remains of the large Guesten Hall can still be viewed in the cathedral's grounds.

Within the grounds of Winchester Cathedral, the Pilgrim's Hall was built during the reign of Edward I (1272–1307). Erected by the monks of St Swithun's priory, its function was to receive pilgrims visiting the saint's shrine. Later such halls came to be located outside the monastic precincts.

In the eighth and ninth centuries, many more hospices were established in response to increased travel. These received and sheltered the pilgrim as 'hospes', or guests. The terminology employed in the development of such provision for the pilgrim tended to blur the intrinsic meaning of different types of establishment. In the ninth century, a *xenodochium* and a hospital tended to imply the same thing, but by the twelfth century, clearer distinctions were drawn between the guesthouse providing board and lodging, and hospitals, themselves charitable institutions, although it was not unusual to stay in a house in which the sick were also catered for.

Hospitals were sometimes founded by knightly orders, such as the Knights Templar, recognised guardians of the pilgrim and the traveller, as well as poorer brotherhoods and those of wealth and influence. Among those founded by military orders were the commanderies established with the same purpose in mind. Some of

Visitors enjoy the traditional Wayfarer's Dole. *John Crook*

Eastbridge Hospital for pilgrims was established on King's Bridge, Canterbury. Becket's nephew Ralph was probably its first Master. The Undercroft, divided into cubicles, was the pilgrims' dormitory. *Master and Trustees of Eastbridge Hospital*

these foundations came to be highly famed and lucrative, preserved under the aegis of the king. The order of Altopascio was one such example, which owned several establishments along the routes to Compostela. Equally, the hospital of St Mary Roncesvalles owned its own network of houses.

In England, the Hospital of St Cross, located just outside Winchester, founded by Henry of Blois, grandson of William the Conqueror, in 1136, was established as an almshouse to which poor pilgrims were welcome. The large hall in which pilgrims ate and slept can still be visited and the traditional 'wayfarer's dole' of a piece of bread and horn cup of ale can be received. Later, in 1445, the Almshouse of Noble Poverty was added for those who had once enjoyed great wealth, but, for whatever reason, had lost it. It is now home to twenty-five brothers who live in the fifteenth-century quarters there.

The Hospital of Saint Nicholas, a mile outside Canterbury in Harbledown, was founded by Archbishop Lanfranc in 1084. As was the usual protocol, pilgrims would be received and invited to kiss the holy relics, and in this instance drink from the holy well. It is often referred to now as the Leper's Hospital, and its sloping floor enabled the building to be flushed out with water more easily after the lepers had attended mass. For those who arrived in England by sea to visit the Canterbury shrine, the Hospital of St John was founded in 1280 at the port of Sandwich.

Henry II is said to have stopped at the hospital in Harbledown before making his penitential crawl to the shrine of Becket. Tradition relates that Erasmus also visited and was presented with a curious relic, a fragment of Thomas Becket's shoe. His companion, Dean Colet, vehemently declined the offer to kiss the shoe and Erasmus was said to have made a generous donation to the hospital to compensate for his companion's outburst.

The area east of London and south of the Thames offered several inns for pilgrims setting out from there for Canterbury, as did Chaucer's pilgrims who assembled at the Tabard Inn at Southwark. There was a chapel to Thomas Becket in the middle of London Bridge, and the Hospital of Saint Bartholomew at Smithfield was a convenient choice of sick pilgrims.

For those poor, weak or sick pilgrims to Canterbury, the Eastbridge or St Thomas's Hospital, as it is also called, was a popular choice. Founded by Archbishop Hubert Walter (1193–1205), visitors can still walk around its Undercroft, the earliest part of the hospital where pilgrims would sleep, the refectory and a pilgrims' chapel. In 1342, Archbishop Stratford expounded the aims of the hospital as:

> for the maintenance of poor pilgrims and other infirm persons resorting
> thither to remain until they are healed of their infirmities; for the poor, persons
> going to Rome, for others coming to Canterbury and needing shelter.[3]

In keeping with these objectives, a revised statute in 1342 stated that the healthy were only to be provisioned with one night's stay, giving priority to poor and sick pilgrims. When Cardinal Pole visited the hospital in the sixteenth century, it had twelve beds, eight for men and four for women. In the reign of Elizabeth I, it was enlarged and a school was added. Since the middle of the sixteenth century the hospital has sponsored two local students a year to attend Corpus Christi College, Cambridge. Today, as with the Hospital of St Cross in Winchester, Eastbridge continues to provide accommodation for the elderly and infirm.

Often, such hospitals provided special burial facilities for pilgrims and foreigners. The Cathedral of St James in Compostela was granted land by the city's archbishop, Gelmirez, in order to facilitate the building of a church as well as the burial of visiting pilgrims and the sick who died there.

Another well-established hospital was set up in 1260 in Maidstone, situated on the main pilgrim's route to Canterbury. Many more such *Domus Dei*, or 'Houses of God', as they came to be known, sprang up along the main pilgrimage routes of Europe.

Naturally, the routes to the main embarkation ports for passage to Jaffa became lined with pilgrim hospices such as those at Marseilles and Venice. The principal crossings of the Alps were also scattered with hospices, notably on the Great and Little St Bernard Passes. The patron of these particular Alpine hospices was their namesake, the eleventh-century cleric, Bernard, who had concerned himself with the safety and protection of pilgrims.

Hostels were institutions which needed to secure a regular income and welcomed donations, legacies and land or building bequests. The eleventh century saw an acceleration in the establishment of hostels founded by merchant communities, Cluniac monasteries and other religious orders. Hostels were founded for different

A lady of the manor offers hospitality to pilgrims. *Cotton Tiberius AVII fol. 90. British Library.*

reasons, whether it be out of reverence in receiving Christ in the pilgrim or as a
military order that gave wealth to the building of hostels and upkeep of roads, even
out of thanksgiving. The hospice at Aubrac was founded in 1100 by a Flemish
nobleman in thanks for his safe return to Compostela after surviving a snowstorm.

Hospice provision varied from region to region, as well between each
establishment. Many hospices did not serve food, while documents show that other
richer establishments were able to provide meat, vegetables and bread, such as at
the Hospice of Pamplona Cathedral. On his own short-lived pilgrimage to Rome,
Reynard the Fox decided to lodge with a friend overnight where he enjoyed salted
meats, cheese and eggs, a rare luxury for the poorer pilgrim. Other institutions
provided alms for the poor pilgrim at their gates. Those offerings given to the
Cathedral at Santiago before terce, the third canonical hour of prayer, on a Sunday
were then extended to the city's lepers.

The *Liber Sancti Jacobi* for pilgrims to Compostela cited three hostels in particular
as worthy of praise.[4] They were those at Jerusalem, the Great St Bernard Pass and
St Christine in the Pyrenees. These were all strategically placed, the Great St Bernard,
for example, being at the highest and bleakest pass of the Alps for the pilgrim.

Founded by Bernard of Aosta, it would have been used by a significant number of French and English pilgrims journeying to Rome.

Positioned on the Somport Pass over the Pyrenees, the origins of the Hospice of St Christine are less detailed. Although it was part of a sequence of hostels provided for the pilgrim through France and Spain on the main routes to Santiago, its position rivalled that of the twelfth-century hospice at Roncevalles located on another principal pass of the Pyrenees and founded by the bishop of Pamplona.

A Latin hospice had existed in Jerusalem since the ninth century, its foundation traditionally attributed to Charlemagne. During unsettled times in the tenth century it fell into abeyance. However, the most famous pilgrim's hospice in Jerusalem, was the Hospital of St John the Baptist, founded by a community of merchants, which existed from around 1060 onwards. It became the headquarters for a crusading order after the capture of Jerusalem in the first crusade in 1095, but still continued to operate as a hospice. Theoderich's description of the hospital in his *Guide to The Holy Land* praises the abundance of provision and space for the accommodation and care of the sick. He estimates that there were over 1,000 beds there, and marks it as a praiseworthy achievement that the hospital was able to operate on such a scale. Unfortunately, this meant that within Jerusalem there was no choice where lodgings were concerned. While laymen were generally housed within the remains of the Crusader Hospital of St John, clerics boarded with the Franciscan community on Mount Sion. It later became a Muslim establishment and Christian pilgrims were charged for the service it provided.

Conditions within medieval hostels varied greatly. Often word was spread by pilgrims themselves, in the form of guidebooks, as to which were better and what to prepare for. One book relates the following exchange between a traveller and his servant who had been sent ahead to check that there: 'be no fleas, nor bugs, nor other vermin'. His reply came: 'no sir . . . for please God you will be well and comfortably lodged there – except that we suffer much from rats and mice'. Another section reveals something of the other problems encountered: 'William, undress and wash your legs and then dry them with a towel and rub them well on account of the fleas, that they may not leap on your legs. For there is a mass of them about in the dust under the rushes. . . . Ow, the fleas bite me so and do me great harm, for I have scratched my shoulders till the blood flows.'[5]

For some, the financial and virtuous rewards encouraged improvisation of accommodation. On Brother Faber's stop in Crete in the fifteenth century, a brothel was converted to an inn in order to accommodate them. In Boccaccio's tale, two young men seek private hospitality at a family cottage. Lodged overnight in the cottage's one bedroom with the husband, wife and two children, the situation arouses inevitable confusion for all concerned and a night of bed-swapping shenanigans ensues![6]

Pilgrims would also lodge at inns, which would also vary greatly in quality and provision, but at the least should have been able to offer guests a bed. It was south of the Thames in London that Chaucer's pilgrims assembled at the Tabard Inn in Southwark before setting off for Canterbury. The remnants of Salisbury's Old George Inn, its medieval gateway and courtyard, now form the entrance to a modern shopping centre. Remains of other medieval inns survive at Gloucester and Glastonbury.

Many inns got away with charging expensive board for low-rate accommodation. A letter from John Paston in 1474 relates such an experience at the George Inn,

Southwark, which left much to be desired. For the more enterprising or experienced pilgrim, other lodgings could be found. Brother Faber hired a villa in Corfu for himself and his companions. It seems that this was a common practice among pilgrims, as Saewulf also writes that he sought out empty huts or cottages, 'since the Greeks did not welcome guests'.[7]

Another popular choice in Canterbury for those that could afford it was the more fashionable Chequer of Hope, conveniently situated on the corner of Mercery Lane and a stone's throw from the gates of Christ Church Cathedral. This is where Chaucer's pilgrims stayed in an epilogue to the *Canterbury Tales*. Its name is a shortening of the chessboard on the barrel (hoop) and perhaps suggests the kind of amusements to be enjoyed there.

> They toke hir In, & loggit hem at mydmorowe, I trowe,
> Atte 'Cheker of the hope', yat many a man doith knowe.[8]

The pilgrim was guaranteed to meet other travellers, from all levels of society and backgrounds at inns and hostels, 'both priests, monks and laymen, gentle and simple, from Germany, from Gaul, and France'. However, innkeepers also had a bad

The Hospitable Pilgrims, relief by Luca della Robbia (1400–82). *Ospedale del Ceppo, Pistoia, Italy/Bridgeman Art Library*

reputation. If one of their guests died, they were known to lay claim to all his or her belongings.[9]

We know from the writings of Faber that the town of Ramleh (en route to Jerusalem from Jaffa) had an inn specifically for Christian pilgrims run by Christians. It had been bought by Phillip, Duke of Burgundy, and was entrusted to the charge of the Franciscan Brethren on Mt Sion. Its surroundings are reminiscent of many larger Arab buildings opening out into a courtyard in the middle.

In most hostels, guests would sleep on straw-covered floors. With so many pilgrims frequenting the same hostels and sleeping on the same floor, there was no reassurance as to how often fresh straw was laid. In general, beds were prized objects owned by those who could afford them. Surviving medieval wills speak of beds, stuffed mattresses, pillows and sheets. In a few cases, such articles were even left to hostels.

Taverns, for those who could afford them, were known for serving better food and were far more likely to have beds. In these instances you could expect to share a bed with at least one other traveller, although the advantages of this do not need to be stated in colder climates. In the jubilee year of 1350, pilgrims paid 13d to share a bed with three others. Men and women would often be offered separate quarters so that even husbands and wives would sleep apart from each other. The Great Bed of Ware, measuring approximately ten feet, nine inches square could sleep twenty!

Competition ensued between inns, hostels and taverns who all vied for supremacy and employed sneaky methods to canvas more customers. Many of them hired boys to rush to the gates of the city to greet, kiss and hug the arriving pilgrims and then lead them back to their respective hostelry. In Compostela, such boys went out wearing or carrying placards that openly advertised their employer's tavern or inn.

CHAPTER TEN

GOD'S MAGIC: SHRINES AND MIRACLES

Many make pilgrimages to various places to visit the relics of the Saints, wondering at the story of their lives and the splendour of their shrines; they view and venerate their bones, covered with silks and gold.[1]

The fundamental importance of the holy shrine was that it was understood, usually through the report of miracles occurring there, that they served to bridge the gap between the banality and suffering of the physical world and the elevated serenity and purity of the spiritual world. The success of these sites as hugely popular visitor attractions relied partly on a readiness to accept the power of the incorporeal world. In the words of one scholar, shrines were 'a locus where heaven and earth met in the person of the dead'.[2] This was coupled with the idea that the workings of the physical world and man's affairs were ordained by God, or else managed by the equally potent satanic influences that were associated with all misfortune. The purpose of this chapter is not to state whether such miracles were genuine or otherwise, but to highlight the circumstances and prevalent beliefs that served as their backdrop.

Among the many shrines visited by pilgrims across Europe were the burial places of early religious martyrs (such as those buried alongside the roads to Rome), those places in the Holy Land directly associated with Christ, as well as non-martyrs' tombs, which included penitents and confessors, or those who had suffered, but not died for their faith. Of the former type, the church at Vézelay was built in memory of the penitent Mary Magdalene. Included in the latter type were those of St Martin at Tours who died at the end of the fourth century and that of Edward the Confessor within Westminster Abbey.

Other churches were set up on the sites of pagan worship and adapted to Christian use, such as St Maria Sopra Minerva in Rome. This church stood on top of the site of a temple to Minerva that had been dedicated by Pompey after his victories in Asia. It was rebuilt in 1370 under Pope Gregory XI and granted to Dominican monks. Other buildings that seem likely to have been sites of pagan worship include St Foy at Conques in France and the present site of the Holy Sepulchre in Jerusalem, which was constructed on the site of a Roman temple.

The Pantheon, Rome, by Bernardo Bellotto (1720–80). *Museum of Fine Arts, Budapest, Hungary/Bridgeman Art Library*

The Pantheon, possibly one of Rome's first pagan temples, was rededicated for Christian worship under Pope Boniface IV in AD 609. Master Gregory in his *Narracio de Mirabilibus Urbis Romae* offers an intriguing insight into this conversion by alluding to the widely held belief that before the rededication, Christians passing the Pantheon were plagued by demons.

As the centre of a saint's cult, such shrines also represented the foundation and heart of the saint's power at its most influential. It is from such sites that God was believed to assert his divine status by channelling the energy to perform holy miracles through his saints. Thus God himself came to be hailed as the most practiced divine *Medicus*, and examples of surviving ampullae promote his holy subject St Thomas Becket as the 'best doctor'. 'O Lord my God, for You are the heavenly Physician of Souls, who both wound and heal, who cast down and raise up again.'[3]

Bede wrote in his history of the English Church that Oswald's great 'devotion and faith' in God during his lifetime was manifested in the miracles that took place after his death. 'For at the place where he was killed fighting for his country against the heathen, sick men and beasts are healed to this day.'[4] It was also possible for God to work his power through living subjects. Bede relates how he warns Bishop Augustine against pride and conceit on hearing that he has been working miracles.

My very dear brother, I hear that Almighty God has worked great wonders through you for the nation which He has chosen. Therefore let your feeling be one of fearful joy and joyful fear at God's heavenly gifts – joy that the souls of the English are being drawn through outward miracles to inward grace.[5]

Pilgrims would worship at the shrines of saints who had performed God's work in their lifetime, and had now been elevated to join with him in divinely influencing the physical world.

Interestingly though, the behaviour of such saints was often seen as being equally judgmental, emotional and prone to ill temper as that of their lesser, mortal beings. One example notes a saint, William of Norwich, clearly exhibiting his need for physical comfort when he appeared to a young girl in her dream to complain that his neck was paining him as he lay in his coffin. In another instance, the prayers of a pilgrim to Canterbury were apparently cruelly ignored by St Thomas on account of the fact that the boy had fallen asleep while offering devotions at his shrine.

The saints did not take kindly to failures to fulfil a particular vow or promise made to them. It was common for people to invoke the help of a saint and make such a promise of either a gift or the undertaking of a pilgrimage if the saint granted their prayer. A tale relates how one knight had vowed to make a pilgrimage to Becket's tomb if his son was cured, but soon came to forget his promise. Another of his sons fell ill and died. Then the knight and his wife became ill. In the understanding that the knight's broken promise was the cause of their maladies, the pair made their journey to Canterbury in order to discharge the knight's vow.

The behaviour of the saints is reminiscent of the portrayal of the gods in Homer's epic poems the *Odyssey* and *Iliad*. Although invested with the power to control every aspect of the physical world from its politics to its weather systems, Homer's Olympian residents were also prone to moments of rage, vulnerability and sometimes lacked compassion for mere mortals. It is certain that the Medieval era did look back to the writings of Greek philosophers and doctors for inspiration and teaching.

Nevertheless, the austere belief in the power and influence of the saints seems never to have wavered in the pilgrim's mind. The physical stance assumed when approaching a revered shrine was often an outward reflection of such a conviction. The pilgrims would adopt a penitential posture from the moment their destination first came into view. For many pilgrims, this meant removing their shoes for the last part of the journey. This was the case at the Slipper Chapel in Houghton St Giles. Here, pilgrims could make their devotions and remove their shoes before walking the last mile of their journey to Walsingham.

On returning from exile in France, Thomas Becket's first sight of Canterbury Cathedral so humbled and inspired him that he walked the remainder of his journey barefoot. Equally, after Becket's murder in the cathedral, Henry II crawled the last two miles of his journey from Harbledown to Canterbury as a gesture of humility and piety in light of the crime committed.

Medieval sources tell us that the pilgrim's first glimpse of Jerusalem from a hill outside the city was a moment of elation and great joy. Suitably this site also became host to the aptly-named Church of *Mons Gaudii*, Montjoie. Surely, this is the church referred to by Theoderich, a German bishop from the thirteenth century, approximately two miles distance from Jerusalem. He relates how pilgrims: 'lay down their crosses and take off their shoes and humbly strive to seek him who deigned, for their sakes, to come there poor and humble'.[6] Even on board ship, the highly emotional and symbolic nature of this occasion was marked. On his way to the Holy Land, Faber describes the moment when the captain called all to the upper deck to behold their first view of the Holy Land. The pilgrims responded in delight singing songs of praise and celebration.[7]

Another example of the physical expression of piety and servitude was the climbing of the Scala Sancta in Rome, which is still revered as the stairway ascended by Christ to meet with Pontius Pilate, miraculously transported to Rome. Catholics still climb it today; it is an awe-inspiring sight to witness as large groups languidly make their way on their knees, step by step, their ascent punctuated with the saying of the Rosary. For the pilgrim this practice is similar to performing the Stations of the Cross in church, or making a tour of Palestine in an attempt to recreate and relive Christ's life and works.

Although it was understood that the venerated figure associated with a shrine was no longer living in the physical sense, such sites were felt to be permeated with the highly charged spiritual energy of that person. This belief offered the desperate, sick, pious or curious pilgrim the chance to exist for a moment in the space and energy of their chosen saint and to experience something of the saint's spiritual aura. Equally, the greater access and proximity allowed, the more profound the energy. Theoderich, in his writings on the Holy Land, described the round hole into which the Holy Cross had been fixed in the Church of the Holy Sepulchre. 'Into this hole pilgrims, out of the love and respect that they bear to him who was crucified, plunge their head and face.'[8] One story relates how a rather large pilgrim to Canterbury managed to climb right inside through one of the niches of St Thomas's first tomb so that he was lying in the small space between the stone coffin and the roof of the shrine. It was proclaimed a miracle that he ever managed to extricate himself.

Some shrines were associated with figures of a more political than religious significance, such as that of Simon de Montfort, Earl of Leicester. Defeated at the Battle of Evesham in 1265, his body was then dismembered by the king's forces. His reputation as a martyr for justice and civil liberty generated an influx of like-minded pilgrims to his burial place at Evesham Abbey from the thirteenth century. Pilgrimage to this site was permitted by Henry III who feared that the miracles that occurred there were a sign of God's veneration of the earl's cause.

The shrine of Thomas Becket also held a political element and stirred much compassion for the saint in the light of his violent end and its apparent injustice. Pilgrims came to 'experience' and contemplate the circumstances surrounding the saint's piety, bravery and martyrdom. In light of such an emotional attachment to a saint, the symbolic significance that was applied to surviving articles of a saint's clothing or physical remains can be understood. Relics served to create a deeper nostalgia and reverence for the saint, as well as allowing pilgrims to experience a greater spiritual proximity with them. Even the earth or sand surrounding a site were felt to be permeated with the energy and potency of the deceased.

Of course, the idea that such holy articles might also hold supernatural power further increased their pulling power. To be the owner of a holy article attached to a venerated figure was one thing, but to be the recipient and subject of that figure's divine healing ability was of the utmost consequence to the pilgrim, particularly as the search for a divinely dispatched cure was one of the driving forces behind many pilgrimages. For a church or monastic house, the possession of a miracle-working relic also held great financial significance.

In their lifetimes important religious figures would be expected to demonstrate generosity and compassion and to dispense spiritual counselling, among other things. Elevated to their seats in heaven, these selfless figures held even greater potential. Worshipping their relics was reported by thousands to have brought healing miracles and signs. This increased the importance of the holy shrine, attracting hoards of pilgrims in search of some relief from their mental or physical suffering.

Profuse emotional and spiritual stirrings are recorded to have occurred at shrines in this way.

In the same way that offerings were left in temples for the ancient Greek and Roman gods, visiting pilgrims would come bearing gifts to be left at the shrine in the hope of securing the saint's intercession. When an illness was cured in this way, a wax effigy of the affected part of the body, or sometimes a donation of wax equal in weight to the sick person would be left. This practice is referred to in the letter of Margaret Paston of Norfolk to her sick husband on 28 September, in about 1443. 'My mother behested another image of wax of the weight of you to Our Lady of Walsingham.'[9]

Alternatively, in the case of disease of the whole body, a wick the length of the person could be coiled up and then waxed to make a 'trindle' candle. On a grander scale, every third year the barons of Dover helped to maintain the shrine at Canterbury in time for the Feast of the Translation on 7 July. A large drum was sent down to the mayor and a long candle stretched around the drum, equal in length to the circumference of the city of Dover. It was then lit every day at the Mass of St Thomas. Another affirmation of this practice tells of a young girl who was rescued from a well in Ifield, not far from Canterbury. She naturally credits Becket with her deliverance on account of the proximity of her accident to the Canterbury shrine and pleads to be measured to St Thomas. A candle equal to the length of the girl was then offered at the saint's shrine.[10] In the thirteenth century Edward I was the proud owner of falcons that he kept caged in a purpose-built mews in the village of Charing. When one of them fell sick, he donated a life-size wax effigy of the ailing bird that he placed in Hereford Cathedral in hopeful dispensation of a cure.

Just as there was a Greek or Roman god assigned to a specific ill or life situation, the pilgrims could implore the governing saint of their particular predicament. Examples included St Radegund for cases of ringworm or toothache, St Giles for leprosy, St Livertin for headaches and St Nicholas for rheumatism or infertility. More directly, the subjects could visit a shrine of the saint associated with their particular ailment to make invocation and offering; for example, many of the healing shrines along the routes to Compostela claimed their own speciality. Lepers could visit the shrine of St Lazare at Autun, while St Hugh of Lincoln's reputation lured those sufferers of toothache. In Whitchurch, Dorset the thirteenth-century shrine of St Candida was associated with healing ailments of the eyes. A mile away to the south of the shrine, the cool waters of a holy well in Candida's name were said to provide a relieving tincture.

The affiliation of saints with particular maladies can partly be attributed to a universal lack of understanding of the physical body. An ecclesiastical ban on dissection further propounded this ignorance. The result was sometimes the perpetuation of beliefs that seem bizarre, even comical to the modern ear, for example the analogy of the human stomach to a kind of cooking cauldron that was kept simmering by the heat of the liver.

The belief that certain foods and beverages served to aggravate particular conditions is not so far from modern thought, but often equally fantastic. Red wine for example was said to enhance a quick temper in all men and should therefore be consumed moderately. Other such beliefs have withstood the test of time, such as redheads having a fiery temper. Medieval thought took this idea a little further, pronouncing that red hair was itself a sign of too much blood in the head, thus causing a discoloration of the hair.

Such a lack of understanding led people to put their faith in mysticism and folk remedies as a means of curing illness. This was strongly disclaimed by the Church that naturally placed the emphasis on sacred rather than profane healing. Furthermore, the Fourth Lateran Council of 1215 urged doctors not to attend to a patient a second time before a priest had visited. Ironically, despite the Church's attitude toward profane healing, many canons, priests, prelates and monks were themselves doctors.

At Canterbury Cathedral there is fascinating material evidence of a continual belief in mysticism – a piece of parchment on which is repeatedly written the incantation 'abracadabra', which can be dated to a third-century Roman doctor. The power of fortune and luck was not underplayed in medieval society, and sometimes pilgrims would leave their choice of saint's shrine to chance in the casting of lots. The most accepted and readily delivered explanation for illness, though, was as a manifestation of the sickness of the soul. Hence the power of holy shrines was promoted as a means for healing.

The physical level at which a saint's bones were placed could also be a relevant factor. The belief that one's social status could be exemplified physically was prevalent in most areas of medieval society, and thus carried over into the spiritual status of saints. For example, when dining the king would be seated at the head of the room on a raised platform known as a dias. This made him clearly distinguishable as the most important person in the room, as well as physically placing him on a higher level than the rest of his guests. The same can be said of modern-day courtroom settings. Equally, thrones or other seats of authority were placed on a dais, often with a footstool or step that raised them to their position of command. In the Old Testament, 1 Kings 10: 19–20, the throne of King Solomon is described as having six steps which led up to its seat.

Just over a decade after the death of St Cuthbert, the brethren at Durham agreed to place the body in a new coffin to be positioned above pavement level as appropriate to the honour the saint merited. St Thomas's shrine at Canterbury was not only raised, but situated at the highest level of the cathedral at the east end, and reached by a flight of steps now known as the 'pilgrims' steps'.

Perhaps the most clearly illustrated example of this practice is in the position of the thirteenth-century shrine of Edward the Confessor. Situated roughly six feet above the pavement, the closest pilgrims could get to his physical remains was to huddle in the niches of the shrine's lower level.

Often, even greater power, prestige and mystique were applied to the shrines by compulsory rituals of cleansing and confession before the pilgrim was considered 'ready' to enter into the presence of the saint and the magical, supernatural energy that radiated from his tomb.

Pilgrims might spend many days, nights, or sometimes weeks at the shrine of a saint, offering their prayers and devotions, often in patient wait for a miracle.

Pilgrims at the shrine of Edward the Confessor in Westminster Abbey, creeping out of apertures that permit them to touch the tomb; a monk supervises the activity. *MS Ee.3.59. By permission of the Syndics of Cambridge University Library*

It would have been a cold, uncomfortable and near desperate experience for some, particularly those with crippling illness. Nevertheless, it seems that they were often welcome to stay as long as they needed, and at Worcester Cathedral charitable arrangements were made by the brethren who laid mats on the floor around the shrine of St Wulstan. Today, one can witness similar scenes at Lourdes, in France, which sees thousands of modern pilgrims arriving, many wheelchair-bound in hope of a modern-day miracle.

It has been suggested that the experience of enduring such conditions in a state of anguished and expectant faith may have produced a placebo effect for some. In this way, the subject would engender a 'self-delivered' psychological cure and leave believing himself the subject of the saint's compassion.

The humbling experience of seeking the forgiveness or aid of a saint was also a socially unifying one. Holy shrines saw visitors ranging from the most destitute of pilgrims, who had funded their journey by begging, to the highest-ranking citizens and their retinues. Perhaps the most famous royal pilgrim is Henry II who sought redemption at the shrine of St Thomas Becket after his men's brutal murder of the bishop in December 1170. Having crawled the last part of his journey from Harbledown just outside Canterbury, he spent the night on the stone floor in front of Becket's tomb. Other royal visitors to holy shrines included Richard the Lionheart to the tomb of Edward the Confessor and Charles VII of France who reportedly went five times to the shrine of the Virgin at Le Puy. Pope Pius II's devotions led him barefoot through the snow to a shrine dedicated to the Virgin in East Lothian.

In some cases, the miracles that occurred at a shrine were recorded for posterity. Those at St Wulstan's shrine at Worcester were logged in about 1240 in the *Miraculi Sancti Wulstani*. In Canterbury two monks collated a list of their saint's miraculous workings. Benedict of Canterbury, who was prior in 1175, was spurred on by a series of visions in early 1171, a year after Becket's murder, and began recording the miracles chronologically. William, another Canterbury monk, started recording in the following year, registering 438 miracles from 1172–79. Between them, Benedict and William recorded 703 miracles in the first ten years after Becket's death.

It is interesting to note that William recorded a proportionately higher number of foreign visitors to the tomb than Benedict, reflecting the fast-spreading power of the cult of St Thomas even between 1171 and 1172. Further evidence of this can be found in medieval art. A mosaic of St Thomas appears in a church at Monreale in Italy, dating from shortly after the martyrdom in the late twelfth century. Becket's shrine in Canterbury received more foreign visitors than any other, with nearly a third of its pilgrims estimated as arriving from outside England.

In Canterbury itself the miracles started very quickly after the death of Becket. One of the earliest recorded concerned a London shoemaker called Gilbert who arrived at the shrine with a weeping ulcer. Ingestion of the Holy Water of St Thomas saw him healed and challenging locals to a foot race to demonstrate his miraculous recovery.

The discussion and exchange of anecdotes concerning miracle cures among village people and travelling pilgrims served to keep the propaganda mill turning. As the saint's cult spread, so his fame grew, and in turn more reported receiving the virtues of his activity. Even biblical stories relating Christ's healing of the sick and the crippled seem to work to this principle. On the occasion that Christ heals a man of a grave skin disorder, he tells him to 'go straight to the priest and let him examine you; then in order to prove to everyone that you are cured, offer the sacrifice that Moses ordered' (Matthew 7: 4). Here, the priest plays a similar role to that of the registrars working at saints' shrines in assessing and authenticating miracle cures. Once the event had been given his seal of approval, the medieval mind could more readily embrace the saint's virtue and supernatural power.

The formula for the establishment of a cult's status was simple. It worked on the receptive mind with one voice or mechanism that enforced the idea (such as a miracle), a small following of subjects to publicise experience of it, and at its most potent, its following is fully receptive and the belief universally cemented in the conscious mind. The response ranges from quietly reverent to reactionary, even hysterical.

Interestingly, villages with which a saint had some intimate tie outside his or her place of burial also experienced miracle activity. For example, as well as Thomas Becket being of Norman descent, France, as the country which had harboured him during his exile, heralded approximately twenty-eight sites of Becket worship. As a result of the archbishop's sojourn in France, he left behind many articles that were then adopted as relics, offering many churches the foundation they needed to establish their own Becket centres. A more tenuous link perhaps was created by the villagers of Newington, west of Canterbury, where Becket had once conducted a

Nicholas of Verdun, engraved gilt and enamelled copper-alloy plaque, SEPVLCRVM DOMINI, showing Joseph of Arimathea and Nicodemus laying the dead Jesus in a sarcophagus. At the front there are three large roundels representing the port holes which were a key feature of the burial couch in the Edicule of the Holy Sepulchre from *c.* 1100 or before until the fourteenth century. From the Klosterneuberg pulpit, completed 1181. *Chorherrenstift Klosterneuberg, Stiftsmuseum/Bridgeman Art Library*

confirmation service. The same emotional and pyschological bonds were established and miracles began to occur there that were credited to Becket's virtue.

Although there is no direct evidence, it also seems likely that there may have been those whose purpose it was to travel the country broadcasting knowledge of a saint's cult, using examples of individuals who had benefited from curative miracles as their drawing power. Certainly there were also some who benefited financially from spreading such gospel in other ways, for example in the selling of fake 'miracle-working' relics.

It was also common for pilgrims to report an experience of a visitation by a saint in a vision or dream. It was in a repeated dream that the widow Richeldis de Faverches was requested by the Virgin Mary to build a church at Walsingham in Norfolk. In the Miracle Windows in Canterbury Cathedral St Thomas is portrayed floating out of his shrine as a suppliant sleeps nearby.

However, not all miracles occurred at the shrine itself. In this respect, Biblical stories create a romantic ideal in their descriptions of instantaneous, spontaneous cures of blindness and paralysis, and it may be easy to comprehend this as having been the reality for medieval pilgrims. In fact, it is thought that roughly half of the reported miracles occurred afterwards within pilgrims' homes and were then reported to the credited saint's shrine at a later date, usually that visited most recently before recovery took place. Equally, cures were not always experienced on the first visit to a shrine, but sometimes on the second, third or fourth visit. In one instance, a leper did not experience a cure until his second visit to the shrine, while other pilgrims made several journeys.[11] Some of these cures from illness or disability also occurred as gradual improvements over time in a way that could be construed as the body's own ability to heal naturally. Equally, though, these were recorded as miracle cures.

This is not to say, however, that the registrars at shrines were prepared to accept and record any cure reported at face value. Often the pilgrim would be required to produce a witness who could testify to the subject's condition before and after the event of the cure. This also helped to eliminate those pilgrims who faked cures in order to gain a moment's notoriety.

The miracle-working shrines of Our Lady at Walsingham and Thomas Cantilupe at Hereford are two centres that came under scrutiny at the Reformation. Walsingham underwent an inquiry in 1535, under Henry VIII, to determine, among other things, the centre's most esteemed relics and the evidence to support they were true. Hereford was subject to the enquiries of papal commissioners in 1307 who scrutinised the procedures used in praying for a miracle at the shrine, how long cures took to manifest and whether there were witnesses to the miracle who could testify to knowing the subject before as well as after the event.

For those pilgrims who were not cured at a shrine, there was little comfort. Many a hermetic explanation was offered to the pilgrim, which usually followed the theory that he had been unworthy in some way, either through lacking faith or belief, or had not carried out a vow sufficiently.

It is interesting to note that in promoting St Thomas Becket as such a masterful healer, the words stamped on many of his ampullae read, *optimus egrorum: medicus fit toma bonorum*, or 'Thomas is the best doctor of the *worthy* sick'.

Individual examples of those who did not receive physical healing at a shrine were sometimes recorded and employed as lessons in faith and worthiness to hopeful

Making medicines, from Roger Frugardi's *Chirurgia*, England, mid-thirteenth century. *Trinity College Cambridge*

supplicants. Such was the case of the mother who took her blind daughter to the shrine of St Wulfstan in Worcester. After three days of waiting in anticipation with no outcome, the mother left the shrine taking her daughter with her, angrily rebuking the saint's proclaimed curative abilities as a farce.[12]

Although pilgrims were usually made to attend confession before approaching a holy shrine, the idea that some pilgrims were denied a cure on account of not confessing their sin was also circulated. It was also proposed that the subject may have fallen victim to a curse pronounced on him by an enemy. Even for the genuinely pious and devout pilgrim, he must have some lurking sin that not even he was aware of.

An alternative explanation was that the afflicted person had been relying on doctors and prescribed medicines rather than seeking divine healing. As one might expect, surviving evidence suggests that many people employed all available help in the event of illness, seeking second opinions from doctors, visiting several different shrines, as well as experimenting with folk medicines. Ultimately though, in the event of healing, there was a readiness to credit a holy saint or divine intervention for their cure.

The failure to receive any sign of restorative cure must have dealt a disheartening, psychological blow to many pilgrims. To have heard tell of others before that had been blessed with a cure and having undertaken a lengthy and treacherous expedition to a site on which they had pinned all hope, must have rendered the blow harsher still, perhaps even resulting in worse illness. It seems likely that many of those who resided at shrines for weeks at a time may have endured there in an unrealistic state of expectation, convinced that their deliverance had to be imminent. The idea that they might not be blessed with a cure was too painful a thought to consider. This may also have partially accounted for those who chose to fabricate their own cures. There were others who in receipt of an apparent cure were then so overwhelmed as to be afraid to leave the shrine in case the illness returned. One such pilgrim cured of his epilepsy resided at Becket's tomb for two years in fear of its return.

Another aspect was the experience of being immersed in an atmosphere of such intense, expectant faith, even hysteria, as to lift the spirits and mental states of all involved. It is in this way that some have proposed pilgrims received deliverance from their illness through a shift in their own psychological state. The maxim 'positive mind, healthy body' rang true then, with the palpable expectation and hope that existed around a shrine perhaps serving to ameliorate the mental prospect and, therefore, physical health of the pilgrim. The power of mass, singular belief and contemplation at a potentially miracle-working shrine is not to be underplayed here.

Many mementos and trinkets were available to the pilgrim as souvenirs. These could be obtained at any of the numerous stalls that were close to the entrance of a shrine in expectation of pilgrim custom. In Canterbury's Mercery Lane, a narrow road leading straight to the entry gate of the cathedral precinct, was the place to buy souvenirs. A guidebook for Santiago de Compostela states that the open square outside the cathedral was the place to buy souvenirs as well as necessities.

In the Holy Land since the sixth century small flasks could be bought by the pilgrim wishing to collect miracle-working water from the Jordan. However, it was the second half of the twelfth century, with its boom in pilgrimage activity, that saw the beginnings of the mass manufacturing of pilgrim souvenirs and badges.

Wherever possible, the pilgrim would endeavour to further substantiate his souvenir by having it blessed at the related shrine, or by bringing it into as close physical contact with the shrine as possible. In this way, it was believed that a portion of the relic's supernatural power would be transmuted to and absorbed by the souvenir.

Notably popular were ampullae or miniature flasks. At Canterbury these small lead phials contained the water of St Thomas Becket. This holy tincture was believed to contain a minute amount of his blood diluted in many more parts water. With great foresight, it seems, the monks at Canterbury had salvaged some of the congealed blood from the stone floor where Becket had fallen. Pilgrims carried the water away from the shrine in their flasks and it was also given to many churches across England, thus further spreading the message of Becket's power.

As a result of its powerful physical association with the martyred saint, the holy tincture became a kind of thaumaturgic talisman for the pilgrim. In this way, souvenirs became perambulatory relics that could be owned and cherished, and the virtues of the saint's curative abilities could be called upon in the comfort of the pilgrim's own home. The beneficial healing properties of the water of St Thomas were usually procured by ingesting it, or applying it directly to the affected part. This is demonstrated in the stained-glass Miracle Windows of Canterbury Cathedral. Recovered ampullae relating to the Canterbury shrine include those of scallop-shell designs, those with rectangular or circular surrounds and others that are shaped like a reliquary chasse, costrel or ship.

In the early Middle Ages many pilgrims managed to acquire the bones of martyrs and saints as souvenirs, though it seems highly probable that many were fakes. For others, fragments of stone or dust from a holy tomb or a handful of earth or dust from a venerated site was sufficient to satisfy the need of pilgrims to own something that could be associated with the saint.

The spot at which King Oswald died in 642 fighting against the heathen Mercians was seen to be of symbolic as well as supernatural significance. Bede describes how people visited and carried away the dust from this site, some mixing it with water in order to create a tonic that was said to benefit the sick.

> This practice became so popular that, as the earth was gradually removed, a pit was left in which a man could stand. . . . Many miracles are reported as having occurred at this spot, or by means of the earth taken from it.[13]

The chipping away of stonework from the Holy Sepulchre in Jerusalem came to be a problem as hundreds of pilgrims sought to claim their souvenir. John Mandeville, a traveller of the fourteenth century, describes the conservation action that authorities were forced to adopt as a result. 'Because some men who went there used to try to break bits of the stone off to take away with them, the Sultan had a wall built round the Tomb so that nobody could touch it except on the left side.'[14] Another pilgrim managed to remove a chunk of stone from the tomb of William of Norwich, which could supply shavings and dust from which to mix numerous curative elixirs.

Important pilgrimage sites often sold souvenir badges that were mostly made of a tin-lead alloy, or brass or clay. They were fitted with a pin or clasp so that the badge could be worn, and the surface was stamped with either a portrait of the saint, a scene from his life or death, or a symbol associated with him. The wolf became the symbol associated with the tomb of St Edmund at Bury St Edmunds. Having been speared and decapitated by the Danes when he refused to renounce his faith, Edmund's head suffered the grievous insult of being hidden in a thicket to prevent it receiving due burial. When it was uncovered, a wolf was found guarding the head from other wild beasts and followed as the head was taken to be suitably buried.

Badges from the shrine of Our Lady of Walsingham naturally portrayed the Virgin, whether it be the statue shown on its own or within an openwork depiction

A wolf guarding St Edmund's head. *Harley MS 2278, f. 64. British Library*

of the Holy House. Also popular were badges showing the anunciation, the earliest of these placing the scene under an architectural canopy.

Pilgrims wore these badges with pride, attaching them to their broad brimmed hats.

> Then, as manere & custome is, signes there they boughte . . .
> They set thir signes oppon thir hedis, & som oppon thir cappe.'[15]

As well as serving as souvenirs, these badges asserted the wearer's status and credentials as a pilgrim and offered visible authentication of his journeys. For some, it seems that there was also an element of competitiveness. The tale of Piers Plowman, written by a fourteenth-century cleric, tells of one pilgrim who is heavily decorated with tokens from his travels. He wears several pilgrim badges on his hat, including phials of holy oil and not just one, but numerous scallop shells. His cloak is also laden with emblems and signs testifying to his trips to Rome and the Holy Land. His objective is clear: 'You can see by the signs in my hat how widely I have travelled – on foot and in all weathers, seeking out shrines of the saints for the good of my soul.'[16]

His self-satisfied attitude and assertion that he has also suffered for his cause are a reminder of the pressures in medieval society to attain the goals of piety and perfection set by the Church. Perhaps it is also an indication of a trade of pilgrim signs among those who wished to prove falsely that they had reached several different pilgrimage destinations.

Some souvenir badges were recovered from the River Stour in Canterbury, but the majority of surviving pilgrims badges were found in the Thames, in London, mostly in the vicinity of

A pewter pilgrim badge of the Virgin and child. *Museum of London*

London Bridge and Blackfriars Bridge. One of the great gathering places for pilgrims was the Tabard Inn at Southwark.

Probably the most well recognised and earliest pilgrim badge was the palm of Jericho symbol which pilgrims brought back from Jerusalem. It is from this symbol of the palm that the name 'palmer' for a professional pilgrim on perpetual pilgrimage came. These palms which were collected in the plain between Jordan and Jericho had associations of regeneration. It is also said that the pilgrims of the first crusade to Jerusalem, in 1095, immersed themselves in the River Jordan and then collected their palms.

The scallop shell, the symbol of Compostela, came to be associated with all pilgrims. Over two hundred shells have been discovered in pilgrim burials dating from the ninth to the seventeenth century from 160 sites around Europe.[17] However, this does not mean that they had all come from Compostela. By the beginning of the twelfth century enterprising businessmen had begun collecting scallop shells for themselves, so that those who had never been to Santiago could also wear its symbol. In response, the archbishops of Compostela attempted to limit the sale of scallop-shell tokens in an effort to retain the emblem's exclusive association with Compostela. By the end of the twelfth century real scallop shells were replaced with a lead badge in the shape of the shell.

Much in the way that the archbishops had fought to preserve the scallop's unique association with St James, Pope Innocent III ruled, in 1199, that the Basilica of St Peter in Rome should have the monopoly over the production of and selling of pilgrim badges showing St Peter and St Paul. Not only would this assure that the canons of St Peter's enjoyed the sole income from the trade, but pilgrims would have to authenticate their ownership of a badge by visiting the basilica first. Other pilgrim-badge symbols from Rome included the holy sudarium at St Peter's. This was a reversed cloth, known as the handkerchief of St Veronica, perhaps from the Latin *vera icon*, or true image, on which the face of Christ that had been miraculously preserved. It grew increasingly in popularity as a pilgrim symbol from the early thirteenth century, and by the fourteenth century St Peter's publicly exhibited the vernicle for pilgrims to see. It not only promised holy miracles, but granted the pilgrim the astounding indulgence of 12,000 years remission for every hour that the pilgrim gazed upon it.

Tokens from Canterbury took many different forms. Some bore the figure of St Thomas wearing his bishop's mitre and holding his crozier, others took the form of a circular disc with the words *caput Thome* around the outside, with the head of St Thomas in the centre. The British Museum has another example that shows Thomas riding on horseback. The gloves of St Thomas were other items of Becket memorabilia that could be bought. Bells could also be purchased at Canterbury to be attached to the pilgrim's clothing or to the bridles of their horses, if they were travelling on horseback. Their relevance seems to lie in the tradition that on the occasion of Becket's death, all the bells of Canterbury rang of their own accord. Also about seventy examples relating to Canterbury have been found at the shrines of Mont-Saint-Michel, Rocamadour and Amiens in France.[18]

Many other pilgrim badges and symbols were made for the prestigious shrines along the routes to Rome, Santiago and Canterbury, as well as others of lesser known and unofficial saints. The shrines of Mont-Saint-Michel, Rocamadour, Saint-Gilles-du-Gard and the Three Kings at Cologne all had their own pilgrim badge symbols, particular to their cult and shrine. Not only do their surviving numbers allow an insight into the popularity of pilgrimage as an established practice in the Middle Ages, but they indicate the systemised arrangement of shrines and their individual significance and interest to the pilgrim.

CHAPTER ELEVEN

DUST AND OLD BONES:
THE ALLURE OF THE HOLY RELIC

So he took away some of the earth wrapped in a linen cloth, thinking that, as the event proved, it might have power to heal the sick.[1]

The recognised physical medium for the generation of holy miracles was the relic. Sometimes this was an object closely associated with the venerated person such as an item of his or her clothing. Frequently though, relics constituted part or all of the person's physical remains. Often these were also believed capable of withstanding the natural processes of decomposition, therefore enhancing their holy prestige.

The most eagerly sought-after relics were those directly associated with the holy family and particularly prized were those articles of the Crucifixion, such as fragments of the crown of thorns, nails, even drops of the Holy Blood. The great Church of St Chapelle in France boasted ownership of the crown of thorns, fragments of the purple cloak of Christ as well as pieces of the True Cross.

Also in heavy circulation were the bones of saints and martyrs. For example, Oswald, Bishop of Worcester and, later, Archbishop of York, had been able to recover some bones of Saxon saints from the ruined Ripon Minster and set them up in a shrine at Worcester in the tenth century. In 1092, his canonisation saw the translation of his own bones to the same reliquary as the Ripon relics.

The quest for the ownership of such relics sometimes led to some extraordinary claims being made. A sixteenth-century French printer, Henry Stephens, recommended one French monastery on account of its glass phial containing Christ's tears and another which held his breath! Hailes Abbey in Gloucestershire claimed its own phial of Christ's blood. It was the power of mass belief, together with an ardent curiosity in the supernatural, that made the worship of these wondrous vestiges of the dead possible. Simultaneously, it made the Church's treasuries rich with the custom of the reverent and inquiring pilgrim.

Great importance came to be placed on all religious buildings being able to offer some vestige of the holy dead on which its visitors could concentrate their devotions. At the start of the seventh century, when St Augustine was peforming his holy vocation in England, Pope Gregory supplied him with all that he felt Augustine

Pilgrims on the Scala Sancta, or Holy Stair, Rome. *John Crook*

would need in order to make his mission successful: 'including sacred vessels, altar coverings, church ornaments, vestments for priests and clergy, relics of the holy Apostles and martyrs, and many books.'[2] Also on Gregory's orders, holy relics were used to replace the idols within the buildings of profane worship as a visual means of establishing Christian worship in England. The explosive propagation of holy relics was perhaps something that Gregory could not have foreseen. His later attempt to discourage the trade in relics included his recounting of a story of a group of men who inadvertently broke into the tomb of St Lawrence. Within a few days of their misdemeanour they all died.

Any opportunity for a church to gather more relics was seized upon with alarming vigour. The aggregation of holy relics was also facilitated by the dismembering of a saint's remains and the dispersal of its parts to a number of different sites. As early as the fifth century, the words of a theologian named Theodoret expounded the accessibility and profligation of holy relics:

> No single tomb covers a martyr's body. Cities and villages, having divided the bodies among themselves, entitle them preservers of their souls and healers, and honour them as guardians of their city. . . . Though the whole body be divided, the grace is undivided, and the smallest relic has equal power with the whole body of the martyr.[3]

Many more relics were brought back to England from the Holy Land by crusaders, where Empress Helena, mother of the Emperor Constantine, had purportedly discovered the True Cross and the Holy Sepulchre on her visit in AD 326. The fall of Constantinople in 1204 saw another influx of bones from the churches of the east. The demand for pieces of the cross was overwhelming, and although some of the cross was said to have made its way straight to Rome, more churches claimed ownership of its fragments than was possible. By 1561, it was disparagingly noted by Calvin that the portions of the True Cross in churches across Europe were enough to load a large ship.[4]

As early as the seventh century the Pope made a generous offering of a rich inventory of relics to Oswy, King of the Northumbrians: 'relics of the blessed Apostles Peter and Paul, and of the holy martyrs Laurence, John and Paul, Gregory and Pancras' and for King Oswy's queen: 'a cross made from the fetters of the blessed apostles Peter and Paul'.[5]

The church attempted to authenticate the seemingly endless traffic of holy articles by endowing them with yet greater mystique and power, the ability of self-multiplication. Conveniently, this theory was often neatly upheld with a citing of the loaves and fishes story in the Bible. The disadvantage of such a notion is highlighted in the account of a pilgrim touring the shrines of France in the sixteenth century. On being introduced to the encased skull of St John the Baptist, he remarked that he had already witnessed it elsewhere at another church.

Both Amiens and Constantinople boasted ownership of the preserved head of John the Baptist. The fourteenth-century English knight, Sir John Mandeville, endeavours to clarify the mystery, explaining that the head was taken to Constantinople by the Emperor Theodosius, still wrapped in its bloody cloth, and that half of it was still there at the time of his travels, while the other half resided at Rome in the Church of St Sylvester. Further to the confusion, though, he states:

'some say that St John's head is at Amyas [Amiens] . . . and some say that that one is the head of Saint John the Bishop. I do not know; God knows.'[6] Highlighting the absurdity of this recurrent confusion one comtemporary churchman commented:

> Some say that they have such and such a relic and others loudly assert that they have it. The citizens of Constantinople claim the head of John the Baptist while the monks of St Jean d'Angely confidently believe that they have it. Now what could be more absurd than to suppose that this great saint had two heads. Let us therefore take this matter seriously and admit that one of them is wrong.[7]

Some relics were obtained by churches through less than honourable means. There are accounts of bishops taking reliquary bones away with them after they had been succeeded, and both Vézelay and St Foy in France, and St Mark's in Venice were in possession of relics that had undergone 'sacred theft' from another church. Equally when Edward I defeated the Welsh he laid claim to their prized relic, a fragment of the True Cross.

An edict of Pope Gregory the Great in the sixth century said that a relic must be housed in a church before the building could be consecrated. Those churches that had already been consecrated and were not in possession of relics were advised to obtain some as soon as possible. Quite simply, there were not enough relics to go around. This led to a flourishing trade in holy articles from the Holy Land, Rome and elsewhere throughout the seventh century, and former regulations protecting the exhumation or dismemberment of the bodies of the dead were rendered redundant. In the eighth century Pope Paul I took to opening up the graves of Rome and donating the contents to those churches unable to abide by his predecessor's edict.

The outcome of this was that England played host to an unseemingly large number of holy relics, which inevitably included those which were fake or 'invented'. As with many trades, opportunists and counterfeiters were at work. It was not beyond them to rob the graves of the dead and sell the exhumed bones to the unsuspecting and the credulous as the authentic remains of a venerated figure. Chaucer's Pardoner chooses animal bones as an resourceful alternative.

> And in a glas he hadde pigges bones.
> But with thise relikes, whan that he fond
> A povre person dwellinge upon lond,
> Upon a day he gat him moore moneye
> Than that the parson gat in monthes tweye.[8]

Aside from an enthusiasm for events supernatural that might offer answers to life's idiosyncracies, it was the ecclesiastical requirement of relics and the re-enactment of Gregory's edict in 787 at the Second Council of Nicaea that facilitated such a trade in holy bones. The Church's justification for the vast number in circulation with the theory of self-profligating relics was apparently readily accepted, perhaps for the deeper supernatural significance it afforded the relics.

The Church also validated the mysterious transportation of holy relics from one site to another. This accounted for the multiple-ownership claims of a single relic.

A reliquiary statue of St Foy from the treasury at Conques Cathedral. *John Crook*

One of the most intriguing examples is the Holy Stair, or Scala Sancta in Rome. Believed to be the marble stairway that Christ climbed in order to come before Pontius Pilate, it had apparently been miraculously transported from Jerusalem to Rome. Likewise the Holy House of Loreto, the reputed home of Jesus at Nazareth, was transported by the hands of angels to its new site in Italy in 1295. A reproduction of the Holy House of Nazareth, in which the Anunciation was believed to have taken place, was constructed on the north coast of Norfolk at Walsingham at the impromptu request of the Virgin who appeared in a dream to a pious widow.

There were those that objected to the near overwhelming importance that came to be attached to the veneration of holy relics. For the main part, such critics felt that this served as a distraction to the pious mind that became overly consumed with curiosity for these physical objects. In 726 Pope Leo had issued an edict denouncing relics, though his stance was taken to be rather extreme and iconoclastic, and therefore rejected by the church.

The majority, though, sought to promote the sanctity and prestige of holy relics; one such was Gregory of Tours who, in the sixth century, embarked on a promotion of their benefits by recording hundreds of relic-related miracles. Much later, in the mid-thirteenth century Thomas Aquinas argued that relics served as a means of bringing people closer to the deceased saint and served as reminders of them. It was understood that such relics were the holy vehicle by which the saint's spirit could channel its power and continue its work in the physical world.

It is certain that the influx and veneration of holy articles caused a sacred, emotional stirring of dynamic proportions. Belief in their magical properties saw layman removing earth, dust and religious tokens from the vicinity of holy shrines, while knights fitted holy relics into the pommels of their swords as holy talismans. The Holy Roman Emperor Charlemagne was said to have obtained one of the nails of the crucifixion which he fastened to his horse's bridle before riding against the Moors.

The usual arrangement for smaller relics was to house them in an ornate, portable casket that could be easily transported or carried in procession. For example, the reliquary of St Foy was processed through the streets of Conques on the occasion of a plague outbreak. Dating from the mid-tenth century, the reliquary shows St Foy seated on a throne made of gold and encrusted gems, and her outstretched arms were used to carry an iron grid, on which she was believed to have been martyred. Another surviving reliquary chasse is of beautifully coloured Limoges enamel illustrating the scene of Becket's martyrdom. It takes the shape of a small building with a roof safely housing the relics within.

Such reliquaries could be made of wood, stone, iron, even gold or silver, and they were often covered with precious stones. Other reliquaries took a more novel approach by assuming the form of the relic stored inside, so that head and arm reliquaries were not uncommon. In the Basilica of St Stephen, in Budapest, preserved and displayed within a jewelled casket is the purported right hand, or 'Holy Dexter' of the State's founder, canonised in 1083.

The growing magnetism and importance of relics meant that churches also made certain adjustments to accommodate them. The altar became the sacred location for the relic. While reliquary shrines were originally kept under the altar, they now became elevated to a position on top of the altar. Soon though, as shrines became

The hand relic, or Holy Dexter, of King Stephen, in the Basilica of St Stephen, Budapest. *Sarah Hopper*

larger and evermore elaborate, the altar became redundant as relics required their own pedestal located behind the altar. The disadvantage of such a location was that it did not allow full access for the visitor.

During the eleventh and twelfth centuries, with the nationwide rebuilding and enlarging of many churches, shrines were finally allowed their own space, often at the east end of the building. At last pilgrims enjoyed easier access to them and were able to walk all the way around them. Abbot Suger claimed that his rebuilding project at St Denis Abbey in the twelfth century was specifically to allow more comfortable access for pilgrims. Indeed, it was in the interest of churches to make the display of their relics as inviting, comfortable and accessible an experience for the pilgrim as possible.

Saint's relics also came to play a fundamental role as sacred objects on which important oaths could be sworn. It was readily understood that the honorary saint would take sincere umbrage if an oath taken in his or her name were to be broken. One tale relates how a man, obviously confident of his own honesty, arrived at court with a small collection of relics instead of a witness. The Bayeux Tapestry shows Harold swearing his allegiance to the Norman King William with each hand placed over a holy shrine. Chaucer's Pardoner endorses his own cause by swearing on the blood of Christ preserved at the Cistercian Abbey of Hailes in Gloucestershire.

The booming trade in relics inevitably led to the circulation of unmarked saint's bones spread over different sites. Consequently, squabbles and uncertainty ensued as to the origins and authenticity of a hoard. There is evidence of the concerns of ecclesiastical centres as to the validity of the relics they were exhibiting. In one case worries were expressed as to whether the right head had been united with the correct body of the decapitated St Edmund of Bury St Edmunds.[9]

During the reign of Edward the Confessor Harold (right) swore an oath at Bayeux that he would accept William, Duke of Normandy, as the next king of England. Detail from the Bayeux Tapestry, before 1082 (wool and embroidery on linen). *Musée de la Tapisserie, Bayeux, France/Bridgeman Art Library*

A reliquiary cask, of gold, lapis lazuli and semi-precious stones, *c.* 1190, containing the remains of Thomas Becket with scenes of his murder. *Private Collection/Bridgeman Art Library*

It seems that inextricably linked to the ownership of relics was a strong element of prestige and snobbery in the desire to assemble the most enviable collection. The forerunners of such activity, and undoubtedly a source of inspiration, were the emperors of Byzantium, whose large collections became dispersed all over western Europe after the Fourth Crusade saw the fall of Constantinople in 1204.

Competitive squabbling is recorded to have flared up between monasteries over the rightful ownership of certain relics. This saw the monks of Poitiers and Tours fighting over the body of St Martin, while Canterbury and Glastonbury found themselves at loggerheads over St Dunstan's remains. As long as pilgrims continued to visit both sites though, the underlying material concerns of both centres would not have been affected.

Sometimes, one way of settling disputes over the ownership of a particular relic was to produce a duplicate. Employing the same belief that pilgrims could benefit from a relic's healing properties by coming into close contact with it, it was understood that the relic's power could also be transmitted to other inanimate objects through close proximity. In this way another head, for example, could be charged with the supernatural energy of the real head of a saint and then be exhibited as a kind of 'secondary' relic. It was perhaps this kind of activity that caused such confusion when a saint seemed to have more than one head! The writings of Gregory of Tour are testimony to the widespread belief in the efficacy of such a practice:

> Should he wish to bring back a relic from the tomb, he carefully weighs a piece of cloth which he then hangs inside the tomb. Then he prays ardently and, if his faith is sufficient, the cloth, once removed from the tomb, will be found to be so full of divine grace that it will be much heavier than before. Thus will he know that his prayers have been granted.[10]

Such handkerchiefs and pieces of cloth were the earliest relics, or *brandea* as they were called, items that had simply been in contact with the saint or his shrine and had therefore become suffused with holiness. The sick woman in Matthew 9: 20–22 was content to touch only the edge of Christ's cloak, certain this would be sufficient to grant her the healing she desired. It is interesting to note that in modern society, celebrities are often greeted by a sea of hands all straining to make physical contact with their idol.

As early as the sixth century, in response to the trade in fake relics, ecclesiastics devised what they believed to be a foolproof method for verifying the authenticity of a questionable relic. It was thrown into a fire: if it was genuine, it should be able to withstand destruction in the heat of the flames.

Further measures were enacted demanding close examination of all relics purported to be authentic. The sixth-century edict that stated that no church be consecrated without the possession of relics was enhanced by a twelfth-century ruling that stated that no church may possess relics unless they had first met with episcopal approval. Pope Innocent III followed suit in 1215 ruling that all relics required the approval of the Roman pontiff.

Europe found itself in the grip of a kind of 'relic frenzy' and, often, the Church's attempts to regulate and control their use passed unregarded by all, not excepting those of ecclesiastical orders who reaped the gains from exhibiting fake relics. Even the Church itself was held up to scrutiny. In Dante's *Inferno*, Popes Boniface VIII, Nicholas III and Clement V are placed in the third valley of Malbolge for simony, as they traded in holy relics, sold indulgences and annulled excommunications. Nicholas III actually mistakes Dante for Boniface VIII whose imminent arrival he is expecting.

> Below my head others have been dragged down
> who are my predecessors in simony . . .
> I shall fall down there likewise, when I see
> The one arrive that I mistook you for . . .
> But I have already been cooking my feet like this
> And been in this place, upside down, for longer
> Than he will be planted here with red feet.

Inferno, Canto XIX, Lines 73–81.[11]

CHAPTER TWELVE

PURCHASING PARDON:
AN EXPLANATION ON INDULGENCES

In church at Assisi, there was exhibited our Lady's kerchief. . . . She was there also on Lammas Day, when there is great pardon with plenary remission.[1]

Throughout the twelfth century the opportunity to receive indulgences became a common driving force behind pilgrimage. Indulgences were formal acts governed by the Church that certified forgiveness for past sins, saving the recipient from a fixed duration in purgatory. Chiefly presided over by the Pope, shrines assumed quantitative value relative to the amount of remission time they offered, so that for example indulgences of up to seven years were available to pilgrims arriving at St Peter's on major feast days.

The accepted medieval view was that all men and women were born sinners and, therefore, purgatory was a certainty after death before the soul was fit for heaven. The prospect struck fear into the medieval heart and its horrors were made very real in the teachings of the Church and medieval art. Naturally, therefore, the opportunity to repair the moral order of one's life and achieve some remission from such a fate was an attractive proposition.

Only a select number of shrines were allowed to dispense indulgences. Many churches in France were charged with this office as a result of Pope Urban II's tour of the country in 1095. The systemisation of indulgences and the time value in indulgences that was offered by different shrines meant that one shrine could hold supremacy over another in offering the greater indulgence. In the same way that religious centres sought to promote the superiority of their collections of relics and the miracles they had performed, those churches to which the papacy granted indulgences had an extra bargaining tool with which to attract pilgrims. In his itineraries for the Holy Land, Wey lists the notable churches and the indulgence they offered as a guide for the pilgrim.

Of the hundreds of churches in existence across Europe, many had been inevitably excluded. For those churches not honoured by the Pope in this way, indulgences were sometimes forged. Also, despite the Pope's overall jurisdiction in this matter, bishops gave themselves the power to dispense indulgences. Smaller local shrines that had been overlooked sought partial indulgences from their

The Jaws of Hell fastened by an angel, from the Winchester Psalter, *c. 1145–55. MS Cotton Nero C IV fol. 39. British Library/Bridgeman Art Library*

bishop, and soon came to offer pilgrims the indulgences associated with the larger, more celebrated shrines.

In 1420, Canterbury declared its own jubilee for the second centenary of Becket's translation, and with it offered plenary indulgence. While such moves helped to put the smaller parish church and shrine back on the map, for the pilgrim, it also meant that he need only make a short, domestic pilgrimage to his local shrine in order to be granted indulgences. Long, arduous journeys were no longer as necessary, and salvation in the form of indulgence could be bought nearly everywhere.

In order to monitor the system and check misuse in the granting of indulgence, the Fourth Lateran Council of 1215 set the forty-day indulgence as the maximum

Christ delivers souls from hell, from the Winchester Bible. *John Crook*

bruno. eodem die inipso monaſ
terio uibente papa tria uttrib'
pmuſ cancelliſ ſacrarunt alta
ria. Tunc papa uñ ſacñdo nuſ
ſaſq; agendo. p alia ſalutiſ hoꝛ
tatita. coꝛd epiſ ᵹ cardinalibuſ
multoꝛq; pſoniſ. ꞏhuicemodi
ſermoꝛem habuit ad pplin.

tutelamq; c
deo et beat
ruſ. romai
Quoꝛ num
me dignati
ſociauit. ꞏn
prioꝛenq; i
domno ac i

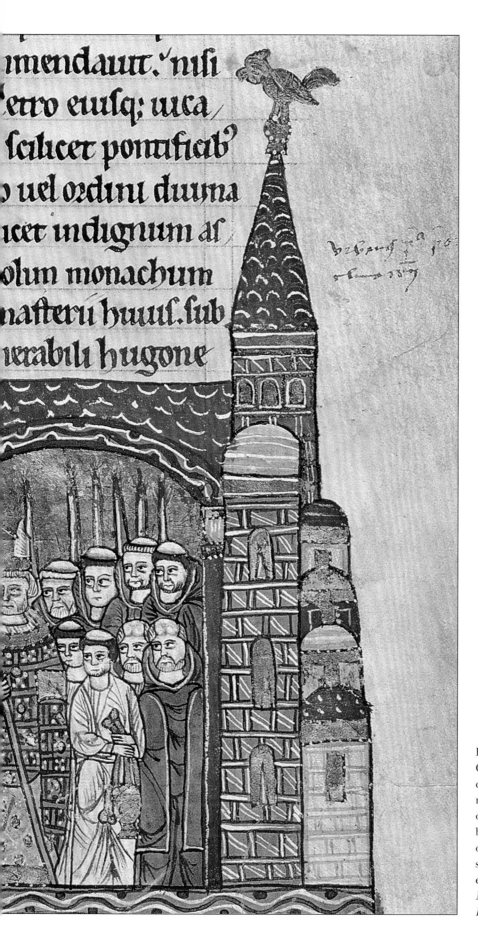

mendauit. nisi
etro eiusq; uica
scilicet pontificab
uel ordini diuina
cet indignum a
olum monachum
nasterii huius. sub
erabili hugone

Pope Urban II on his way to Clermont. The Pope (left) consecrates the high altar of the new church of the abbey at Cluny on 25 October 1095, three weeks before the opening of the Council of Clermont. Abbot Hugh of Cluny stands with his monks at the other end of the altar. *Bibliothèque Nationale, Paris/Bridgeman Art Library*

The traffic in indulgences in a sixteenth-century engraving.

that bishops could grant. It imposed new parameters within which the bishops had to operate as a way of controlling the superfluous sale of indulgences. For example, bishops could not issue indulgences of more than forty days for the feast of a patron saint. While this checked the power that the bishops had in this matter, by the end of the thirteenth century, the distribution of indulgences became more widespread as Popes became more generous by making them available at every church in Rome.

Perhaps the most memorable and vivid portrayal of purgatory is in the drawings of Botticelli for Dante's *Purgatory*. This journey through limbo uncovers a multitude of cruel torments wherein each sins is assigned its own agonising penalty. The lustful are purged in fire, the wrathful are forced to supplant their fury with praise of God, the prideful bear great racks on their backs and the eyes of the envious are sewn up with wire. Even the Pope is held up to scrutiny.

Before indulgences became available, penance could be paid in one's lifetime through a chosen punishment deemed equal to the weight of the sin. In the seventh century Theodore, Archbishop of Canterbury, stipulated that the penance for a man who got himself drunk and vomited was a fast of bread, salt and water for fifteen days. For a priest who found himself in the same predicament, the period was extended to forty days of fasting.

The gravity of the sin committed could be lightened by performing good deeds, and going on a pilgrimage was one such act. It was in the seventh century that the notion that such penitential acts could work to reduce the amount of time spent in purgatory was derived. It was only later that collecting indulgences at shrines became the penitent's tangible assurance of his period of remission.

Aside from partial indulgences, which released the sinner from a fixed period of time in purgatory, plenary indulgences were also available that granted *full* remittance from all penitential suffering. Such complete remission was offered to those who agreed to leave their homes and take up arms in foreign lands in the name of the cross, to join a crusade. Such crusaders were considered as 'armed pilgrims'. Pope Urban II offered the first of such plenary indulgences at the Council of Clermont in 1095. He stated that all those who joined the army on the first crusade to Jerusalem to enforce Christianity and liberate the Holy Land from the grip of the Saracens would receive remittance for their entire penance. Logically though, it was only fair that a greater part of the sinner's penance be erased, as his chances of an early death were greatly enhanced.

For the duration of the year 1300, Rome's first jubilee year, Boniface VIII offered plenary indulgence to all those visiting the basilicas of SS Peter and Paul in Rome. For pilgrims from abroad a sojourn of fifteen days was required, although Boniface's bull indicated that the indulgence was further substantiated if the pilgrim were to extend his pious duty at the holy places. It has been suggested that the immense impact of Rome's jubilee year on pilgrim attendance was partly due to the misleading wording of the bull itself. Pilgrims interpreted the indulgence as offering an expiation of their sin, as well as of their penance in purgatory. The Bull promises 'not only full and complete, but the most total forgiveness for all their sins'.[2] When challenged, it was stated that the indulgence pronounced only that the penitents be as free of guilt and sin as the day they were baptised.

Although the jubilee was originally announced as a centenary celebration, Boniface's successor, Pope Clement VI, yielded to pressure and made it every fifty years. The next jubilee was to be held in 1350. Pilgrims were also required to visit the Basilica of St John in the Lateran, as well as those of Peter and Paul, and then they would receive the fullest forgiveness of all their sins.

At around this time, the Church seemingly came to realise that it was not in the best position to be judging the weight of a man's sin in order to discern appropriate punishment. In many instances, a man's sin much outweighed any punishment that could be prescribed, which would amount to infinite years in purgatory. Equally, there was no penitential deed sufficient that was humanly possible to eradicate man's sin. It was understood that in order to establish an equilibrium between man's crimes and his pious deeds, more efficacious deeds were required. Such deeds and merits were not within the capacity of mortal men; they were the saintly merits of Christ, the Virgin and the saints.

These saintly virtues were 'stored' in the 'Treasury of Merits', and were called upon to substantiate the penance of the sinner as necessary. It was held that the merits and good deeds of these holy figures were infinite, so that the treasury could never be exhausted. For good measure though, the Church said that as the merits were used up, more would manifest themselves to fill their place, a theory strongly reminiscent of the notion attached to the self-multiplication of holy relics.

Satan presides over the torments of the damned in hell, detail from the tympanum of the west portal of Conques Cathedral. *John Crook*

The wicked are devoured by beasts, Aulnay church, France. *John Crook*

Pope Clement VI gave his explanation concerning this supernatural stockpile of sacred virtues. He described the treasury as:

> not one that is deposited in a strong room, or concealed in a field, but which is to be successfully distributed to the faithful through the blessed Peter, keeper of Heaven's gate, and his successors.

He also reassured that there need be:

> no fear of an absorption or a diminution of this treasury, first on account of the infinite merits of Christ, as has been said before, than because the more

Matthew Paris's drawing of the Sudarium of St Veronica in his *Historia Anglorum. MS 16:53v. The Masters and Fellows of Corpus Christi College, Cambridge*

numerous are the people reclaimed through the use of its contents, the more it is augmented by the addition of their merits.[3]

For those pilgrims who died or met with some genuine impediment, either en route to Rome or while performing their duties in Rome, some allowances were made. These pilgrims, if truly penitent, would still receive their indulgence. Clement VI later retracted this though, in the case of the sick, elderly and infirm, for whom other arrangements for indulgence could be made. Increasing the opportunity for more pilgrims to benefit from such indulgence, in 1470 the celebration of the jubilee was increased to every twenty-five years. Again, though, conditions of the jubilee indulgence of 1350 became confused by word of mouth and inaccurate renderings of the original Unigenitus of Clement VI. Many such false bulls influenced the hopes and interpretations of pilgrims.

One such version was recorded by one Albericus de Rosate, which increased the pilgrim circuit to include the Basilica of Santa Maria Maggiore, San Lorenzo Fuori le Mura, Santa Croce in Gerusalemme and San Sebastiano, although these had long been on the pilgrim's itinerary. He also added a visit to see the sudarium of St Veronica. On seeing it he states that the effect of the indulgence would be divinely conveyed upon the pilgrim. Clement VI's original bull does mention the holy image of Christ, but only in terms of the image preserved in the Lateran.

As time went on, the importance of going on pilgrimage to benefit from indulgence began to dissipate. The sick or elderly, for example, could send money to a shrine of their choice, or else pay someone to go in their place. In this way, the merits of the journey and a visit to the shrine were still felt to be conferred upon the subject. Special concessions were being made to royalty and indeed to the whole island of Mallorca (for a payment of 30,000 florins), whereupon the merits of indulgence were conferred upon them as if they had made the journey to Rome. In the tenth century a religious council at Rheims had allowed similar privileges to those who chose to abstain from a crusading expedition, but donated offerings of money instead. Later such monies would come to be collected from those who had been unable to attend Rome for the 1475 jubilee and used to fund a war against the Ottoman Turks.

Of course, the Church at Rome benefited greatly from the offerings and payments of those pilgrims arriving in Rome, as well as those who sent proxies and sums of money. In 1394 Boniface IX granted the city of Cologne its own indulgence, whereby pilgrims could benefit from visiting the city's many relic-holding churches, as well as its great cathedral. It is interesting to note that while the offerings of pilgrims were conceded to Cologne's churches, the Pope still claimed a portion of the payments sent by those who could not make the journey to Cologne for the upkeep of the churches in Rome.

The quantitative apportioning of indulgences to holy sites came to assume a meaningless and unsystematic arrangement, whereby Rome's indulgences were of greater value than those of the Holy Land, while the pilgrimage to Rome offered the pilgrim the lighter, less arduous journey. The idea that a pilgrimage's efficacy lay in the spiritual as well as physical endurance it comprised had come to hold no meaning. In some cases, the pilgrim need not leave his home at all. In other respects it also introduced the notion that only the poor, who could not afford to

Chaucer's Pardoner from the *Canterbury Tales*, fifteenth century manuscript. *Huntingdon Library and Art Gallery, San Marino, California, USA/Bridgeman Art Library*

hire proxies or send gifts of money, need undertake the risks of a pilgrimage, particularly in light of Clement VI's affording full indulgence to King Edward III and his family without their being required to journey to Rome.

The sale of indulgences was later to be used as a point of discussion by those who re-evaluated the efficacy of pilgrimage. In the fifteenth century Erasmus' 'Rash Vows' highlighted the way in which the accessibility of indulgences devalued the purpose of seeking spiritual atonement when pardon could be thus purchased. When asked how he could be sure that the relaxed, pious attitude of his companion who died on pilgrimage had admitted him to heaven, a returning pilgrim replies, 'because he had a purse bulging with the most generous indulgences'.[4]

Equally, as with the money brought in by holy relics, the sale of indulgences often coincided suspiciously with increased outgoing expenditure by a religious centre. Nowhere is this better demonstrated than in Rome, which earned itself a reputation with contemporary critics for misuse of the sale of indulgences. Martin Luther criticised Pope Leo X for the profits he procured through indulgence sales to complete the building work at St Peter's. Luther was so moved to anger that he devised a scathing attack on the church's methods concerning indulgences, consisting of ninety-five points of discussion.

As with the trade in fake relics, the sale of unauthorised indulgences became rife. Despite preventative measures, such as Bishop Grandisson of Exeter's ban on the sale of such bogus pardons within his diocese, the credulous and unsuspecting were preyed upon by those of less than virtuous morals. A pardoner assumed the characteristics of a self-proclaimed ecclesiastic dealer in indulgences.

The pardoner's role entailed travelling the country retailing the 'merits' and relics of saints and martyrs, in exchange for worldly goods and gifts to be donated to the seat of the Catholic Church in Rome. Much to the consternation of the Church in Rome, many such pardoners had set themselves up without ecclesiastic authority, carrying fake licences and working under the pretext of having been granted the mission by the Pope. There was much to be gained from this practice, as all profits made from the sale of fake relics and pardons were often kept by the pardoner instead of being given to the Church.

In his description of a group of pilgrims in *Piers the Plowman*, William Langland takes time to focus on the crooked traits of the pardoner. His document is adorned with suspiciously prominent bishop's seals that the pardoner pushes in the faces of the ignorant and unsuspecting. Won over with his promises of absolution, his audience are ensnared while he 'raked in their rings and jewellery with his roll of parchment!'[5]

Chaucer's pardoner appeared to be particularly good at his job by way of his deceptive and commanding nature. He is described as having a voice as loud as a bell that captures the attention of his victims, preaching with heavy irony on the goodness of heaven and moral virtues. He employs wild gesticulations of his arms and has wide, staring eyes that flash about or keep an intense gaze, holding his audience captive. He carries a pillowcase which he exhibits as the Virgin's veil and his relics were pig's bones! In one day, such deception would earn him as much money as many made in three months.

> And thus, with feyned flaterie and japes,
> He made the person and the peple his apes.[6]

CHAPTER THIRTEEN

OPPOSITION TO PILGRIMAGE

The name of religion is used as a cover for superstition, faithlessness, foolishness, and recklessness.[1]

Pilgrimage played an integral and fundamental part in Christian life throughout the Middle Ages. It was a custom that saw a massive increase in travel, trade and a more transient society. While the Church promoted pilgrimage as a pious means of recommending the soul to God at any of a number of holy shrines, it also introduced the opportunity to escape the routine of everyday life, which brought with it inevitable consequences. 'Men are often moved by curiosity and the urge for sight-seeing, and one seldom hears that any amendment of life results.'[2]

An increasing number of pilgrims came to consider pilgrimage as an excuse for a spring excursion. It offered the chance to get away, meet new people, experience new cultures and witness places that they had only ever heard about, in the words of Chaucer himself, 'to seken straunge strondes [shores]', and to enjoy 'felawshipe' with others.[3]

Brother Felix Faber confessed to making a second pilgrimage to the Holy Land for the simple reason that he enjoyed it. Ironically, on seeking advice before his first pilgrimage, he had also been warned about those many pilgrims who were motivated by 'frivolity or curiosity, having as their object the pomps of this world, or any other empty and transitory vanities'.[4] The Canons of Hereford devised a form of sabbatical system to control the undertaking of pilgrimage within their orders. Subjects were restricted to only one overseas pilgrimage in their lifetime. Equally, time limits were imposed on the pilgrimages they did make: three weeks for those within England, four months for Rome or Santiago and a year for Jerusalem.[5]

The fourteenth-century writings of Sir John Mandeville, a knight errant who claimed to have travelled as far as China, were circulating in Europe from 1356. They served as a chocolate box of tantalising disclosures of the cultures, customs and concerns of foreign lands. They shared intriguing details of trees that bore honey and wine, races that had but one eye in the middle of their foreheads, as well as more orthodox information on the routes to Jerusalem and the customs of the Saracens. Mandeville also emphasised the significance of the holy city's location. 'It is a commonplace that Jerusalem is in the middle of the earth; it may be proved thus.'[6]

A fourteenth-century marginal painting showing a Dominican and a Franciscan monk from *De Pauperie Salvatoris*, by the Bishop of Armagh, a treatise on ecclesiastic poverty including abuse by wandering friars. *MS 180, fil. 1r. The Masters and Fellows of Corpus Christi, College, Cambridge*

With such information as this in circulation, as well as the tales of fellow villagers returning from pilgrimage, the awakening of an urge and curiosity for things outside one's normal environment can be understood. Pilgrimage provided the endorsed pretext needed for a withdrawal from the domestic and repetitive nature of the monthly schedule, to be immersed in new surroundings and experience.

Even if such urges were not the original driving force for the pilgrim, undoubtedly profane distractions would inevitably reach him en route. Once in foreign lands, the pious reason for his journey may have taken second place to the novelty of his new surroundings. Hearing sermons, offering of devotions and collecting indulgences may have become a more mechanical impulse for some.

From early on there were expressed doubts as to the efficacy of people leaving their domestic responsibilities in pursuit of a God that was just as accessible from home. In the fourth century St Jerome wrote of his concern at the neglecting of everyday duties in favour of pilgrimage to the Holy Land. However, the idea that

God could be more present in one place than another was prevalent in the medieval psyche, and for pilgrims it had come to be understood that the opportunity to venerate the sites of Christ's Passion was paramount to bring themselves closer to God. As a permanent resident in Jerusalem, Jerome confessed that he felt no more praiseworthy or pious for living there, with the message that salvation could be more effectively sought at home through inner contemplation than by the undertaking of pilgrimages.

Other critics were concerned with the exploitation of pilgrimage as a religious act and the corruption and iniquity it engendered among some of its participants. Contrary to the Church's ideal, Thomas à Kempis commented that pilgrimage rarely brought the pilgrim spiritually closer to God. Perhaps most concerning was the fact that those of religious orders were also succumbing to varying levels of temptation and vice through pilgrimage. Bishop Faber recorded his sea journey to the Holy Land in the fifteenth century and noted the gambling, swearing and blaspheming that took place on board. He singles out the Bishop of Orléans as a particularly zealous gambler. On this occasion though, piety prevailed and the decision to ban all games of dice or cards was taken.[7]

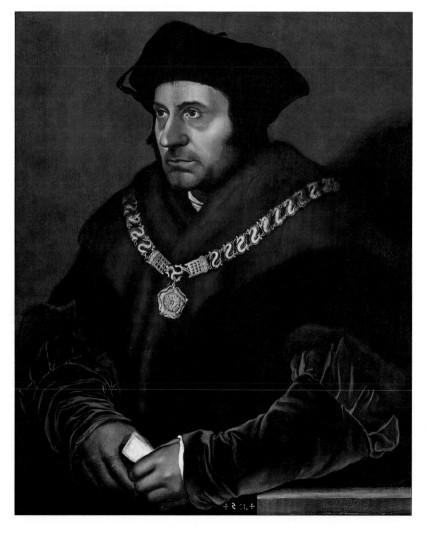

Thomas More, by Hans Holbein the Younger (1497/8–1543). *Philip Mould, Historical Portraits/Bridgeman Art Library*

Of the eight ecclesiastical figures in Chaucer's merry band, the majority readily succumbed to a neglecting of their duties, while others used their position to exploit the trusting layperson. Their victims seem mostly unsuspecting that a man of ecclesiastical orders would take their money and gifts for anything other than religious means, although for Chaucer to be writing about it, corruption within religious orders must have been a well-recognised phenomenon. Of the monk he says, 'Is likned til a fissh that is waterlees – This is to seyn, a monk out of his cloistre'.[8] In fact, nearly all of Chaucer's pilgrims exhibit a lack of moral values and spiritual discipline. In their quest for social pleasure and entertainment, Chaucer's band make up a rather boisterous and rowdy troop. At the time Chaucer was writing, *c.* 1380–1400, pilgrimage was experiencing the advanced process of its decline, and its practice had come to assume far less spiritual motives.

Detail from a sixteenth-century woodcut showing John Knox. *C37 d.47 bi. fii. British Library/Bridgeman Art Library*

Another contemporary writer, the cleric William Langland, voiced his criticism of the part played by the religious orders in bringing pilgrimage into disrepute through corrupt example. 'I saw Friars there too – all four orders of them – preaching to the people for what they could get. In their greed for fine clothes, they interpreted the Scriptures to suit themselves and their patrons.'[9]

The end of the crusades had made travelling to the Holy Land far more difficult. As a result, pilgrimage became more popularly concerned with local shrines, and domestic pilgrimage within England increased. Psychologically, shorter journeys were more comfortable and therefore treated far less as an arduous, penitential journey, and were more readily regarded as a leisurely outing.

Much anti-pilgrimage invective is found in Thomas More's *Dyalogue on the Adoracion of Images*. It speaks of those pilgrims whose incentives were void of piety and motivated by the chance to socialise and get drunk with new-found companions. Other critics included Lollard heretics such as William Thorpe.

I know well that when divers men and women will go thus after their own wills, and finding out one pilgrimage they will ordain beforehand to have with them both men and women that can well sing wanton songs. And some other pilgrims will have them bagpipes so that every town that they come through shall know of their coming, what with the noise of their singing and the sound of their piping, what with the jangling of their Canterbury bells, and the barking out of dogs after them. They make more noise than if the King came there away with all his clarions and many other minstrels.[10]

In 1407 William Thorpe was tried for heresy by the archbishop of Canterbury for highlighting such ways in which he saw pilgrimage being abused. He stated that in visiting such sites as Canterbury and Walsingham men were disserving God by wasting money and forming relations with lascivious women. Archbishop Arundel could only defend the practice by reminding Thorpe of the many 'great and praisable miracles' that had also taken place at such sites of worship.[11]

Female pilgrims were readily targeted by some critics for particular scrutiny. Saint Boniface (680–754) exclaimed that women making pilgrimage often sacrificed their virtue in so doing. Centuries later, Thomas More was highlighting the inappropriate behaviour of female pilgrims who sang wanton songs along the way. Chaucer's Wife of Bath is a colourfully rendered example of a woman who thrived on the adventure of pilgrimage. Her record is an impressive one with three separate visits to the Holy Land, as well as journeys to Rome, Bologna, Compostela and Cologne. In his heavily ironic fashion, Chaucer the Pilgrim tells us 'She koulde muchel of wandringe by the weye'.[12]

Not only does she dress in a way as to provoke the lustful eye of her company with scarlet hose and visible garter, she is socially vivacious and skilled in the art of love potions and the finding of husbands, of which she has had five. It was probably this kind of conduct, so poignantly portrayed by Chaucer, that prompted disquiet in the minds of some and provided ammunition for 'anti-pilgrimage' critics.

The other side of this was that pilgrimage could also be a more dangerous pursuit for women. Geoffrey de la Tour warned his own daughters against it and Christine de Pisan, who wrote a kind of behavioural handbook for ladies in the fourteenth century, followed the same line of advice for her audience. In so doing, she employs another notion that was popularly cited by censurers of pilgrimage, that the money expended on pilgrimage could be put to better use elsewhere. 'Nor should she go off on these pilgrimages got up for no good reason and involving a lot of needless expense.'[13]

In the thirteenth century the Franciscan preacher, Berthold of Regensburg (1210–72), had also highlighted this point stating that often this use of funds was made at the expense of the family and children left behind. An exchange between a returning pilgrim and his friend highlight the lasting nature of this concern in Erasmus's later fifteenth-century *Rash Vows*:[14]

Cornelius	'You don't return holier?' [from Jerusalem]
Arnold	'Oh, no; worse in every respect.'
Cornelius	'Richer, then?'
Arnold	'No – purse emptier than an old snakeskin.'

Bernard of Clairvaux (1090–1153) had criticised another financial aspect of pilgrimage – the clerical profiteering and suppositional greed of the Church. He opposed the excessive expenditure on shrines and the overly lavish decoration that pilgrimage had afforded many churches. He seemed to recognise that the greater the pilgrimage custom received by a particular shrine, the more embellished and the higher its claims as a pilgrimage centre became, and thus it had more power to draw further pilgrims.

In so far as the treatment of female pilgrims was concerned, Margery Kempe offers a first-hand, fifteenth-century account of the disrespectful behaviour endured from some male companions. She is taunted for her orthodox piety, stolen from and eventually abandoned. At the same time though, it was in the best interests of safety to be travelling with other pilgrims, even if, for the most part, these were men. Discovered by a band of poorer pilgrims, they are astonished to find her travelling alone and thus she is accepted into new pilgrim company.[15]

A misericord of Satan inciting two women to gossip in church, Ely Cathedral.

Criticism of the licentious behaviour of some pilgrims and the adoption of vices while on pilgrimage were well founded, and testified to by many. In the memoirs of Arnold von Harff, a well-travelled pilgrim of the fifteenth century, is included a list of useful phrases, though not always of a nature one might deem necessary, such as 'Madam, shall I marry you?', 'Madam, shall I sleep with you?' and 'Good woman, I am already in your bed!'[16] Thomas à Kempis highlights such behaviour less categorically: 'Those who make frequent pilgrimage seldom acquire holiness by so doing.'[17]

The experience of Margery Kempe reflects the divide that existed between those pilgrims, like herself, that truly believed in the efficacy of their journey and who tried to fulfill it in fully devotional spirit, and the adventure-bound who sought other excitement from their journey.

The fourteenth-century provincial cleric, William Langland, who wrote the spiritual allegory, *Piers the Ploughman*, is very direct in his own criticism of pilgrims. His writing highlights the aspect of camaraderie and profane competitiveness among the pilgrims, as opposed to any spiritual contemplation of the shrines they had witnessed.

And I saw pilgrims and palmers banding together to visit the shrines at Rome and Compostela. They went on with their way full of clever talk, and took leave

Desiderius Erasmus, by Quentin Massys (*c.* 1466–1530). Inspired in part by the spectacle of selling both indulgences and church offices, he argued for a return to a simple church that was based primarily on faith and charity. *Palazzo Barberini, Rome/Bridgeman Art Library*

to tell fibs about it for the rest of their lives. And some I heard spinning such yarns of the shrines they had visited, you could tell by the way they talked that their tongues were more tuned to lying than telling the truth, no matter what tale they told.[18]

A century earlier, Berthold of Regensburg in his *Two and Twenty Virtues* noted that the topic of one's experiences on pilgrimage had become the subject of idle chatter in the church pews. He also asserts God's authority over the power of the saints in Rome or Compostela as omnipotent and as readily available to the layman in his own backyard as at the end of a pilgrimage expedition.[19]

Many writers and preachers feared the dangers of idolatry and superstition. Such tensions concerning the worship of relics had begun in the Church as early as the fourth century. Again it raised the issue of undertaking costly pilgrimages inspired by an urge for sightseeing when God's glory could be felt in any church by taking mass and communion. Thomas More wrote his *Dyalogue on the Adoracion of Images* in order to expound his own misgivings. St Bernard of Clairvaux (1090–1153), John Wycliff, the fourteenth-century leader of the Lollards, and Erasmus (*c.* 1466–1536) were others who voiced anxiety about the mystique and adoration attached to saints and their relics. Thomas à Kempis commented that

> they view and venerate their bones, covered with silks and gold . . . and one seldom hears that any amendment of life results . . . but here in the sacrament of the altar, You are wholly present my God.[20]

Although the part played by relics was generally understood by such critics, some were concerned by the distraction that their excessive adulation served in diverting the pilgrim's attentions from God. This is neatly exemplified by Margery Kempe when she encounters a woman returning from Jerusalem who carried an image of Christ in a chest. When presenting it to other women in the cities she passed through, she dressed it up in shirts and lavished it with kisses, worshipping it with great reverence, as though it had been God himself.[21]

By the fourteenth century John Wycliff had also taken a vociferous stand against the power of the Pope to proclaim a man a saint, discounting Becket as a holy martyr and denying the virtues of miracle-working relics. After his death in 1384 his followers, the Lollards, continued the cause throughout the fifteenth century. His writing on images and pilgrimages argued that those visiting holy shrines had come to attach all 'marvellous and precious works' to images of God and the holy family, these having been man-made to the design of the pilgrim's common imagination, 'the Father as an old man, and the Son as a young man on a cross'.[22] His criticism employed the common line of argument of those revoking the excessive worship of relics, namely that the figure of God himself became overlooked in the mist of such misplaced devotion. This was later reflected in the admonitions of John Calvin (1509–64). 'When Christ ought to have been sought in his word, sacraments and spiritual influences, the world, after its wont, clung to his garments, vests and swaddling clothes.'[23] Equally, the circulation of fake relics continued to cause confusion and consternation among those who revoked their excessive worship. Calvin highlighted the risk of pouring devotions and reverence on bones that could as easily be those of a dog, horse or a thief, or venerating an article attributed to the Virgin that belonged to a prostitute.

The popularity of shrines had been underpinned by the belief in the supernatural power of relics and holy images. To the consternation of Thomas More pilgrims were travelling long distances to channel their devotional energies into a relic or a shrine when the spiritual nature of God or a deceased saint was omnipresent. Pilgrims and laymen, on the other hand, attached physical manifestations to a saint that only occurred in a particular place, usually a shrine. In some instances, different manifestations of a holy figure could occur at different places, so that the pilgrim could journey to different parts of England to visit Our Lady of Walsingham or Our Lady of Ipswich.

Others went so far as to point to the use of fake contrivances which fooled the expectant pilgrims into the belief that they had witnessed a divine marvel, such as a statue of the Virgin that shed real tears. The overseers of would-be pilgrimage sites were also held up to scrutiny: 'Some priest to bring up a pilgrimage in his parish, may devise some false fellow feigning himself to come and seek a saint in his church and there suddenly say that he hath gooten his sight. Then ye shall have bells rung for a miracle, and the fond folk of the country soon made fools.'[24]

Shrines and pilgrimage faced their ultimate challenge in the sixteenth century with the wholesale rejection of all relics, images and indulgences. Henry VIII's (1509–47) destruction of holy shrines and the Dissolution of the monasteries broke the backbone of the pilgrimage tradition. As far as can be discovered, 563 monasteries were dissolved and roughly 9,000 monks and nuns were poorly pensioned off. Having appointed himself head of the Church, any person or thing deemed a threat to his complete supremacy over State and Church was exposed and terminated, this included the dead.

Thomas Becket, by this time a venerated saint, served only as a reminder to Henry of the kind of opposition that could prove dangerous. Henry ruthlessly ordered the destruction of St Thomas's shrine and his holy bones were scattered. He also ordered that any existing images of the saint within his kingdom be destroyed and stated that Becket should no longer be referred to as a saint. Anyone that persisted in worshipping St Thomas would be found guilty of idolatry and thrown in jail. Information from copies of the Treasurer's Rolls at Canterbury give a clear indication of how the cult of Becket declined with the progression of the sixteenth century. A note in one of the sacrist's books before the destruction at Canterbury records that offerings to all the altars in Canterbury Cathedral in the year 1532 amounted to no more than £13 13s 3d. It is doubtful that the previous jubilee of 1520 was even celebrated there. Other saints also bore the brunt of Henry's new agenda as he assumed the authority to undo the Pope's work in revoking the sainthood of many canonised figures.

The effects on pilgrimage were at first drastic and seemingly irreparable. However, as long as people continued to seek forgiveness and spiritual atonement, there would always be a place for holy shrines, saints, relics and all things interpreted as paths to God. After the Reformation, pilgrimage continued to be practised on the continent by Roman Catholics and Orthodox Christians.

CHAPTER FOURTEEN

CONCLUSION

If only from the many avenues of enquiry that it poses, it is clear that pilgrimage was one of the most influential and crucial aspects of medieval society. Aside from its roots as a prescribed exercise of piety, pilgrimage permeated many other strands of contemporary life. It influenced sickness and death with the employment of hired pilgrims by the frail and on behalf of the dead as requested in wills. It played its part in law enforcement as an act of penance and helped to shape a more established interpretation of sin and purgatory, implanting a more urgent need for redemption in the hearts of many.

From a social viewpoint, pilgrimage expanded the vision of the medieval layman in terms of the possibilities outside his domicile or country and the opportunity for travel and new experience. Emotionally, and practically it affected the family unit with those left at home enduring the long absences of family members away on religious pilgrimage.

Medieval pilgrimage served to further the transient nature of its society, witnessing the dissemination of different cults, as well as literature and art that became flavoured with the cultures and tales of foreign lands. Geographically, it raised the profile of many towns and villages in England and on the continent that had previously been lesser known, such as Little Walsingham. Simultaneously, it tested the resilience and resources of larger cities such as Rome in the wake of heightened pilgrimage activity.

Commercially, it created increased opportunity for those who enterprisingly sought to gain from the practice of pilgrimage. Taverners, souvenir vendors, ship owners, thieves and relic fraudsters alike all profited. For the Church also, while promoting the active atonement of sin and the veneration of the saints, pilgrimage served to increase its own financial resources.

For many the practice of pilgrimage satisfied a deep need to repair the spiritual and moral order of their life. It offered the opportunity to recommend oneself to God in the commended and fashionable way and earn some assurance of peace after death. In admitting the layman to the privilege of visiting sacred places, pilgrimage also advanced the interpretation of the ethereal world. In a society that already accepted the existence of satanic forces and fantastic beasts, the belief in divinely orchestrated miracles was intrinsic to the pilgrim's evaluation of the holy shrine.

From early on, pilgrimage also received its share of criticism from those concerned by the dangers of idolatry, and profane motives which compromised moral values, and indeed by those who grew tired of the disruptive nature of pilgrims passing through their villages and towns. Pilgrimage met its greatest challenge, though, with the Reformation. Nonetheless, its value and significance was not eradicated with Henry VIII's destruction of shrines and monasteries. The Reformation saw only its temporary supression while the idea of pilgrimage remained powerful to the Protestant faith and continued to be practised by Roman Catholics on the continent. Today, the impulse to visit those shrines of important saints and to seek cures and miracles persists. Holy sites such as Lourdes, Walsingham and Croagh Patrick receive significant numbers of visitors each year, motivated by faith, curiosity or otherwise. While no longer prescribed as an act essential to spiritual health, the modern pilgrim continues to seek his or her own salvation, rejuvenation and fulfilment through pilgrimage. Many of the same benefits are derived and it is cherished for the memories and unique experience it offers.

Die Jacobs Bruder make their way to Compostela, dressed in the traditional pilgrim's garb ornamented with scallop shells. Jost Amman, *Panoplium omnium artium*, 1568 (hand coloured). *Mary Evans Picture Library*

NOTES

CHAPTER ONE

1. Bede, *A History of the English Church and People*, trans. Leo Sherley-Price, Harmondsworth, 1972, bk V, ch 7, pp. 280–1.
2. Theoderich, *Guide to the Holy Land*, trans. A. Stewart, New York, 1986, prologue, p. 1.
3. J. Wilkinson, *Jerusalem Pilgrimage 1099–1185*, London, 1988, p. 94.
4. T. à Kempis, *The Imitation of Christ*, London, 1984, p. 86.
5. A. Dante, *La Vita Nuova*, trans. B. Reynolds, London, 1978, p. 97.
6. T. à Kempis, *The Imitation of Christ*, London, 1984, p. 58.
7. *Ibid.*, p. 59.
8. *Ibid.*, p. 68.
9. Bede, *A History of the English Church and People*.
10. C. de Pisan, *The Treasure of the City of Ladies*, London, 1985, p. 168.
11. G.G. Coulton, *Medieval Panorama*, Cambridge, 1938, p. 405.
12. John XXII, *Communes*, 5, no. 55710, as cited in D. Webb, p. 104.
13. D. Webb, *Pilgrims and Pilgrimage in the Medieval West*, New York, 1999, p. 58.
14. *Ibid.*, pp. 52–3.
15. G. Chaucer, General Prologue to the *Canterbury Tales*, ed. J. Winny, Cambridge, 1989, lns 1–2, p. 12.
16. D.J. Hall, *English Medieval Pilgrimage*, London, 1965, p. 111.
17. T. à Kempis, *The Imitation of Christ*, p. 105.

CHAPTER TWO

1. *Travels of Sir John Mandeville*, London, 1983, p. 91.
2. Theoderich, *Guide to the Holy Land*, pt I, XII, p. 19.
3. *Book of Margery Kempe*, trans. B.A. Windeatt, London, 1994, p. 60.
4. W. Wey, *Itineraries to Jerusalem, 1458*, Roxburgh Club, 1857, p. 7.
5. While Faber is familiar to many as Brother Fabri, this mistake is an error due to the adoption of this name as it appears at the beginning of the manuscript when stating that the work is of 'Fabri' (using the Latin dative ending in 'i'). In this book he will be referred to as Faber.
6. *Book of Margery Kempe*, p. 103.
7. *Travels of Sir John Mandeville*, p. 77.
8. *Itinerary of Bernard the Wise*, AD 870, trans. J.H. Bernard, London, 1893, pp. 11–16.
9. *Travels of Sir John Mandeville*, p. 78.
10. *Saewulf – Pilgrimage to Jerusalem and the Holy Land*, p. 10, trans. The Lord Bishop of Clifton, Palestine Pilgrims Text Society 4, reprint, New York, AMS Press, 1971.
11. Theodosius, *On the Topography of the Holy Land*, trans. J.H. Bernard. London, 1893, pp. 40–5.
12. Theoderich, *Guide to the Holy Land*, pt II, XXI, p. 35.
13. *Book of Margery Kempe*, p. 104.
14. W. Wey, *Itineraries to Jerusalem*, p. 14.
15. *Ibid.*, p. 7.

16. *Egeria's Travels in the Holy Land*, trans.
J. Wilkinson, Warminster, UK, 1981, p. 21.

17. Lambert of Hersfield, *Annales*, Monumenta
Germaniae Historiae, Scriptores, 5,
pp. 168–9, as cited in D. Webb, p. 43.

18. *Travels of Sir John Mandeville*, p. 80.

19. *Book of Margery Kempe*, p. 111.

20. *Wanderings of Brother Felix Fabri*, trans.
A. Stewart, London, 1893, I, p. 341.

21. *Travels of Sir John Mandeville*, p. 77.

22. W. Wey, *Itineraries to Jerusalem*, p. 7.

23. *Book of Margery Kempe*, p. 110.

24. W. Wey, *Itineraries to Jerusalem*, p. 7.

CHAPTER THREE

1. Master Gregorius, *Narracio de Mirabilibus
Urbis Romae*, London, 1986, ch. 1.

2. *Good News Bible*, United Bible Societies,
London, 1994, Acts 19:21.

3. W. Wey, *Itineraries to Jerusalem,*
pp. 143–8.

4. C.P. Thiede and M. D'Ancona, *The Quest for
the True Cross*, London, 2000.

5. *Book of Margery Kempe*, p. 268.

6. J. Capgrave, *Ye Solace of Pilgrimes*, Oxford,
1911, p. 73.

7. Master Gregorius, *Narracio de Mirabilibus
Urbis Romae*, ch. 4.

8. *Ibid.*, ch. 27.

9. C. Hibbert, *Rome, Biography of a City*, New
York, 1985, p. 92.

10. Records suggest that about 2 million people
arrived in Rome for the jubilee of 1300.

11. J. Capgrave, *Ye Solace of Pilgrimes*, p. 63.

12. Giovanni Villani, *Nuova Cronica*, ed. G. Porta,
Florence, 1990–1, 2, pp. 37–8, as cited in
D. Webb, p. 117.

13. *Book of Margery Kempe*, p. 115.

14. *Chronicon Adae de Usk, 1377–1421*, trans.
C. Given-Wilson, Oxford, 1977, p. 171.

15. *Ibid.*, p. 161.

CHAPTER FOUR

1. P. Coehlo, *The Pilgrimage*, London, 1997,
p. 12.

2. *Le Guide du Pèlerin de Saint Jacques de
Compostele*, Mâcon, 1950 (bk 5 of the *Codex
Calixtenus*).

3. L. Lubin, *The Worcester Pilgrim*, Worcester
Cathedral Publications, 1990.

4. *Ibid.*, bk 5, ch. 9.

CHAPTER FIVE

1. Gervase, *On the Burning and Repair of the
Church of Canterbury in the Year 1174*, ed.
C. Cotton, 1930, pp. 10–11.

2. All in window niii of the Becket windows in
the Trinity chapel, Christ Church Cathedral,
Canterbury.

3. Gervase, *On the Burning and Repair of the
Church of Canterbury*, p. 11.

4. D.H. Turner, 'The Customary of the
Shrine of St Thomas Becket', *Canterbury
Cathedral Chronicle*, no. 70, 1976,
pp. 16–22.

5. Figures cited in C. Woodruff, 'The Financial
Aspect of the Cult of St Thomas of
Canterbury', in *Archaeologia Cantiana*, vol. 44,
1932, pp. 13–32.

CHAPTER SIX

1. J. Adair, and P. Chèze-Brown, *The
Pilgrim's Way: Shrines and Saints in
Britain and Ireland*, Hampshire, 1978,
p. 120.

2. D. Erasmus, *Pilgrimages to Saint Mary of
Walsingham and Saint Thomas of
Canterbury*, trans. J.G. Nichols, London,
1849, p. 13.

3. *Ibid.*, p. 23.

4. *Ibid.*, p. 26.

5. J. Adair, and P. Chèze-Brown, *The Pilgrim's
Way*, p. 120.

CHAPTER SEVEN

1. *Romance of Reynard the Fox*, trans. D.D.R.
Owen, Oxford, 1994, p. 142.

2. *Sarum Missal in English*, Church Press Co.,
London, 1968, p. 548.

3. J. Toulmin Smith, *English Guilds*, Oxford, 1870, p. 157.

4. G. Chaucer, General Prologue to the *Canterbury Tales*, ed. J. Winny, Cambridge, 1989, lns 105–8.

5. *Ibid.*, lns 457, 441 and 566.

6. *Wanderings of Brother Felix Fabri*, vol. vii, p. 3.

7. J.J. Jusserand, *English Wayfaring Life in the Middle Ages*, London, 1950, p. 223.

8. Theoderich, *Guide to the Holy Land*, New York, 1986, pt iii, xxviii, p. 46.

9. *Ibid.*, pt i, xvii, p. 31.

CHAPTER EIGHT

1. Sir Walter Raleigh, *The Passionate Man's Pilgrimage*, in *Elizabethan Verse*, ed. Edward Lucie-Smith, Harmondsworth, 1986, p. 208.

2. Pilgrims on foot generally covered between fifteen and thirty miles a day.

3. Constantinople also claimed ownership of the head of John the Baptist.

4. *Calendars of Patent Rolls*, ed. II 1, p. 76, as cited in D. Webb, *Pilgrims and Pilgrimage in the Medieval West*, p. 171.

5. *Le Guide du Pèlerin de Saint Jacques de Compostelle*, trans. J. Mâcon Vieillard, 1950, ch. 7, p. 21.

6. W. Stubbs, *Seventeen Lectures*, Oxford, 1886, p. vi, p. 128.

7. *Chronicon Adae de Usk, 1377–1421*, trans. C. Given-Wilson, Oxford, 1997, p. 155.

8. Bede, *History of the English Church and People*, bk 4, ch. 1, p. 203.

9. W. Wey, *Itineraries to Jerusalem*, p. 5.

10. *Le Guide du Pèlerin de Saint Jacques de Compostelle*, ch. vii, p. 27 and 29.

11. S. Heath, *Pilgrim Life in the Middle Ages*, London, 1911, pp. 155–6.

12. *Book of Margery Kempe*, pp. 282–3.

13. *Ibid.*, p.144.

14. *Wanderings of Brother Felix Fabri*, intro., vol. vii, p. 87.

15. *Ibid.*, p. 23.

16. Rymer's, *Foedera*, ed. T.D. Hardy, 1704, vol. ii, p. 468 and 12, 1434, vol. x, pp. 567–9.

17. *The Wanderings of Brother Felix Fabri*, intro., vol. vii, p. 157.

18. *Ibid.*, p. 121.

19. *Ibid.*, p. 145.

20. *Ibid.*, p. 97.

21. W. Wey, *Itineraries to Jerusalem*, p. 4.

22. *Ibid.*, p. 4.

23. *Book of Margery Kempe*, p. 281.

24. *Le Guide du Pèlerin de Saint Jacques de Compostelle*, p. 15.

25. W. Wey, *Itineraries to Jerusalem*, p. 6.

26. *Pastons in Medieval Britain*, ed. M. Whittock, Oxford, 1993, p. 44.

27. *Ibid.*, p. 44.

28. G.G. King, *Way of St James*, New York and London, 1920, bk 1, p. 134.
    You who are going to Saint James
    I humbly implore you
    Have no haste:
    Go gently,
    Ah! How the poor sick are suffering
    And many a man and woman
    dead along the way.

29. *Wanderings of Brother Felix Fabri*, intro. vol. vii, p. 9.

30. *Ibid.*, p. 190.

31. *Book of Margery Kempe*, p. 102.

32. *Ibid.*, p. 105.

33. *Ibid.*, p. 281.

34. *Ibid.*, p. 285.

35. Pietro Azario, *Liber Gestorum in Lombardia*, RIS 16, iv, pp. 93–4, as cited in D. Webb, p. 249.

36. E. de Certain, *Les Miracles de Saint Benoît*, Paris, 1858, pp. 64–5, as cited in D. Webb, p. 33.

37. *Book of Margery Kempe*, p. 110 and 278.

38. Wilkinson, *Jerusalem Pilgrims Before the Crusades*, Warminster, 1977, letter 108, pp. 47–52.

CHAPTER NINE

1. Syn Isenbras in E.V. Utterson, *Early Popular Poetry*, London, 1817, I.

2. Matthew 10: 40–2.

3. With thanks to the Eastbridge Hospital, Canterbury.

4. J. Vieillard, *Le Guide du Pèlerin de Saint Jacques de Compostelle*, ch. 4, p. 11.
5. J. Sumption, *Pilgrimage: An Image of Medieval Religion*, New Jersey, 1975, p. 202.
6. Boccaccio, *Decameron*, trans. G.H. McWilliam, London, 1972, ninth day, sixth story.
7. J. Wilkinson, *Jerusalem Pilgrimage 1099–1185*, London, 1988, p. 99.
8. *Tale of Beryn*, ed. F.J. Furnivall and W.G. Stone, New York, 1981; Prologue to the *Canterbury Tales*, lns 13–14.
9. *The Book of Wanderings of Brother Felix Fabri*, intro., vol. vii, p. 11.

CHAPTER TEN

1. T. à Kempis, *The Imitation of Christ*, p. 186.
2. P.R.L. Brown, *Relics and Social Status in the Age of Gregory of Tours*, University of Reading, 1977, p. 4.
3. T. à Kempis, *The Imitation of Christ*, p. 163.
4. Bede, *History of the English Church and People*, bk 3, ch. 9, p. 156.
5. *Ibid.*, bk 1, ch. 31, p. 88.
6. Theoderich, *Guide to the Holy Land*, pp. 59–60.
7. *Wanderings of Brother Felix Fabri*, intro., vol. VII, pp. 207–8.
8. Theoderich, *Guide to the Holy Land*, pt I, XII, p. 20.
9. *Paston Letters*, ed. Norman Davis, Oxford University Press, 1963, p. 6.
10. R.C. Finucane, *Miracles and Pilgrims. Popular Beliefs in Medieval England*, 1977, ch. 8, p. 95, n. 46.
11. J.C. Robertson, ed., *Materials for the History of Thomas Becket*, 1875–85, pt I, pp. 330, 339 and pt II, p. 150.
12. R.C. Finucane, *Miracles and Pilgrims*, p. 79, n. 56, p. 227.
13. Bede, *History of the English Church and People*, bk 3, ch. 9, p. 156.
14. *Travels of Sir John Mandeville*, trans. C.W.R.D. Moseley, Harmondsworth, 1987, ch. 10, p. 77.
15. *Tale of Beryn*, Prologue to the *Canterbury Tales*, lns 170, 190–1.
16. William Langland, *Piers the Ploughman*, trans. J.F. Goodridge, London, 1966, p. 77.
17. H. Lubin, *Worcester Pilgrim*, Worcester Cathedral, 1990, pp. 25–7.
18. H. Spencer, *Pilgrim Souvenirs and Secular Badges*, Museum of London, 1998, p. 123.

CHAPTER ELEVEN

1. Bede, *History of the English Church and People*, ch. 10, p. 157.
2. *Ibid.*, p. 85.
3. J.A. MacCulloch, *Medieval Faith and Fable*, London, 1932, p. 121.
4. J. Calvin, *An Admonition Concerning Relics*, Buckinghamshire, 1995, p. 5.
5. Bede, *History of the English Church and People*, p. 200.
6. *Travels of Sir John Mandeville*, trans. C.W.R.D. Moseley, p. 92.
7. Guibert of Nogent, *De Pignoribus Sanctorum*, p. clvi, lns 607–80, as cited in J. Sumption, p. 27.
8. Chaucer, Prologue to the *Canterbury Tales*, ed. J. Winny, Cambridge, 1989, lns 702–10.
9. *Chronicle of Jocelin of Brakeland*, ed. H. Butler, London, 1949, p. 114.
10. J. Sumption, *Pilgrimage: An Image of Medieval Religion*, p. 24.
11. Dante, A. *The Divine Comedy*, trans. C.H. Sisson, Oxford, 1998.

CHAPTER TWELVE

1. *Book of Margery Kempe*, p. 115.
2. *Les Registres de Boniface VIII*, ed. G. Digard, 4 vols, Paris, 1907–39, n. 3875, as cited in D. Webb, p. 76.
3. J.J. Jusserand, *English Wayfaring Life in the Middle Ages*, p. 176.
4. D. Erasmus, *Colloquies*, trans. C.R. Thompson, p. 7.
5. W. Langland, *Piers the Plowman*, trans. J.F. Goodridge, London, 1966, p. 27.
6. G. Chaucer, The Prologue to the *Canterbury Tales*, 708–9.

CHAPTER THIRTEEN

1. D. Erasmus, *Colloquies*, p. 626.
2. T. à Kempis, *Imitation of Christ*, p. 186.
3. Prologue to the *Canterbury Tales*, ln 13.
4. *Wanderings of Brother Felix Fabri*, intro., vol. vii, p. 4.
5. A. Kendall, *Medieval Pilgrims*, London, 1986, p. 21.
6. *Travels of Sir John Mandeville*, pp. 131, 137, 129.
7. *Wanderings of Brother Felix Fabri*, intro., vol. VII.
8. G. Chaucer, Prologue to the *Canterbury Tales*, lns 180–1.
9. W. Langland, *Piers the Plowman*, p. 26.
10. D. Erasmus, *Pilgrimages to Saint Mary of Walsingham and Saint Thomas of Canterbury*.
11. *Ibid*.
12. G. Chaucer, Prologue to the *Canterbury Tales*, ln 469.
13. C. de Pisan, *Treasure of the City of Ladies*, trans. S. Lawson, London, 1985, part II, ch. 8, p. 168.
14. D. Erasmus, *Colloquies*, p. 4–7.
15. *Book of Margery Kempe*, pp. 280–1.
16. J. Sumption, *Pilgrimage: An Image of Medieval Religion*, p. 195.
17. T. à Kempis, *Imitation of Christ*, p. 58.
18. W. Langland, *Piers the Plowman*, p. 26.
19. D. Webb, *Pilgrims and Pilgrimage in the Medieval West*, London, 1999, p. 239.
20. T. à Kempis, *Imitation of Christ*, p. 186.
21. *Book of Margery Kempe*, p. 113.
22. A. Hudson, *English Wycliffite Writings*, Cambridge, 1981, ch. 12, p. 16, lns 6–7.
23. J. Calvin, *An Admonition Concerning Relics*, Buckinghamshire, 1995, p. 2.
24. J. Sumption, *Pilgrimage: An Image of Medieval Religion*, p. 55.

BIBLIOGRAPHY

Adair, J. and Chèze-Brown, P., *The Pilgrim's Way*, Hampshire, 1978.

Alexander, J. and Binski, P., *Age of Chivalry – Art in Plantagenet England 1200–1400*, London, 1987.

Alexander, P., *The Life and Letters of Paul*, Hertfordshire, 1984.

Biddle, M., *The Tomb of Christ*, Stroud, 1999.

Brodrick, J., *Saint Ignatius Loyola, The Pilgrim Years*, London, 1956.

Brown, P.R.L., *Relics and Social Status in the Age of Gregory of Tours*, University of Reading, 1977.

Butler, H., ed., *The Chronicle of Jocelin of Brakeland*, London, 1949.

Church Press Company, *Sarum Missal in English*, London, 1968.

Coelho, P., *The Pilgrimage*, London, 1997.

Coulton, G.G., *Medieval Panorama*, Cambridge, 1938.

Darlington, R.R., ed., *Vita Wulfstani of William of Malmesbury*, London, 1928.

Davidson, L.K. and Dunn-Wood, M., *Pilgrimage in the Middle Ages – A Research Guide*, New York, 1993.

Finucane, R.C., *Miracles and Pilgrims. Popular Beliefs in Medieval England*, 1977.

Geary, P.J., *Furta Sacra: Theft of Relics in the Central Middle Ages*, Princeton, U.P., 1978.

Gervase, *Of the Burning and Repair of the Church of Canterbury in the Year 1174*, ed. Charles Cotton,
    Friends of Canterbury Cathedral, 1930.

Hall, D.J., *English Medieval Pilgrimage*, London, 1965.

Heath, S., *Pilgrim Life in the Middle Ages*, London, 1911.

Hibbert, C., *Rome, The Biography of a City*, New York, 1985.

Jusserand, J.J., *English Wayfaring Life in the Middle Ages*, London, 1950.

Kendall, A., *Medieval Pilgrims*, London, 1986.

King, G.G., *The Way of St James*, New York and London, 1920.

Lubin, L., *The Worcester Pilgrim*, Worcester Cathedral Publications, 1990.

MacCulloch, J.A., *Medieval Faith and Fable*, London, 1932.

Mancinelli, F., *The Catacombs of Rome: and the Origins of Christianity*, Scala, Florence, 1981.

Morton, H.V., *In Search of the Holy Land*, London, 1979.

Ohler, N., *The Medieval Traveller*, trans. C. Hillier, Suffolk, 1989.

Oursel, R., *Les Pèlerins du Moyen Age*, Paris, 1963.

Parks, G.B., *The English Traveller to Italy*, Rome, 1954.

Peters, F.E., *Jerusalem – The Holy City in the Eyes of Chroniclers, Visitors, Pilgrims and Prophets From the Days of
    Abraham to the Beginnings of Modern Times*, Princeton, 1985.

Prescott, H.F.M., *Jerusalem Journey: Pilgrimage to the Holy Land in the Fifteenth Century*, London, 1954.

Reader, I. and Walter, T., ed., *Pilgrimage in Popular Culture*, London, 1993.

Robertson, J.C., ed., *Materials for the History of Thomas Becket*, 1875–85.

Spencer, B., *Pilgrim Souvenirs and Popular Badges*, Museum of London, 1998.

Stopford, J., ed., *Pilgrimage Explored*, York, 1999.

Stubbs, W., *Seventeen Lectures*, Oxford, 1886.

Sumption, J., *Pilgrimage: An Image of Medieval Religion*, New Jersey, 1975.

Tate, B. and Tate, M., *The Pilgrim Route to Santiago*, Oxford, 1987.

Thiede, C.P. and D'Ancona, M., *The Quest for the True Cross*, London, 2000.

Toulmin Smith, J., *English Guilds*, Oxford, 1870.

Turner, D.H., 'The Customary of the Shrine of St Thomas Becket', *Canterbury Cathedral Chronicle*, no. 70, 1976.

Utterson, E.V., *Early Popular Poetry*, London, 1817.

Vieillard, J., trans., *Le Guide du Pèlerin de Saint Jacques de Compostelle*, Mâcon, 1950.

Webb, D., *Pilgrims and Pilgrimage in the Medieval West*, London, 1999.

Wilkinson, J., *Jerusalem Pilgrimage 1099–1185*, London, 1988.

——, *Jerusalem Pilgrims Before the Crusades*, Warminster, 1977.

Woodruff, C.E., 'The Financial Aspect of the Shrine of St Thomas of Canterbury', *Archaeolgia Cantiana*, vol. 44, 1932.

Zacher, C.K., *Curiosity and Pilgrimage: The Literature of Fourteenth-Century Discovery in England*, Baltimore, 1976.

MEDIEVAL AND EARLY TEXTS

Bede, *History of the English Church and People*, trans. L. Sherley-Price and R.E. Latham, London, 1975.

Bernard the Wise, *The Itinerary of Bernard the Wise (AD 870)*, trans. J.H. Bernard, London, 1893.

Calvin, J., *An Admonition Concerning Relics*, Buckinghamshire, 1995.

Capgrave, J., *Ye Solace of Pilgrimes*, eds Mills and Bannister, Oxford, 1911.

Chaucer, G., General Prologue to the *Canterbury Tales*, ed. J. Winny, Cambridge, 1989.

Chronicon Adae de Usk, 1377–1421, trans. C. Given-Wilson, Oxford, 1997.

——, *The Divine Comedy*, trans. C.H. Sisson, Oxford, 1998.

Dante, A., *La Vita Nuova*, trans. Barbara Reynolds, Harmondsworth, 1969.

de Pisan, C., *The Treasure of the City of Ladies*, trans. Sarah Lawson, UK, 1985.

Egeria: Diary of a Pilgrimage, trans. G.E. Gingras, USA, 1970.

Egeria's Travels in the Holy Land, trans. J. Wilkinson, Warminster, 1981.

English Wycliffite Writings, intro., Anne Hudson, ch. 16: 'Images and Pilgrimages', Cambridge, 1978.

Erasmus, D., *Pilgrimages to St Mary of Walsingham and St Thomas of Canterbury*, trans. J.G. Nichols.

——, *Colloquies*, trans. C.R. Thompson, UK, 1965.

Hadewijch, *The Complete Works*, trans. C. Hart, New York, 1980.

Information for Pilgrims Unto the Holy Land, ed. E. Gordon Duff, Lawrence & Bullen, London, 1893. (Reproduction of the book printed by Wynken de Worde in 1498, 1515 and 1524, based on information from the works of William Wey.)

Josephus, *The Complete Works*, trans. William A.M. Whiston, Nashville, Tennessee, 1998.

Kempis, T. à , *The Imitation of Christ*, trans. L. Sherley-Price, UK, 1984.

Langland, W., *Piers the Ploughman*, trans. J.F. Goodridge, London, 1966.

Master Gregorius, *Narracio de Mirabilibus Urbis Romae*, trans. J. Osborne, Pontifical Institute of Medieval Studies, Canada, 1987.

Materials for the History of Thomas Becket, ed. J.C. Robertson, vol 1, London, 1875–85.

Memorials of Saint Dunstan, Rolls Series 63, pp. 391–5 (for Sigeric's account).

Peter Idley's 'Instructions To His Son', ed. C.D. Evelyn, Boston, 1935.

The Book of Margery Kempe, trans. B.A. Windeatt, London, 1985.

The Book of Wanderings of Brother Felix Fabri, trans. A. Stewart, London Palestine Pilgrims Text Society, 1887–97.

The Paston Letters, ed. Norman Davis, Oxford University Press, 1963.

The Romance of Reynard the Fox, trans. D.D.R. Owen, Oxford, 1994.

The Song of Roland, trans. Dorothy Sayers, Harmondsworth, 1971.

The Tale of Beryn, ed. F.J. Furnivall and W.G. Stone, New York, 1981.

The Travels of Sir John Mandeville, trans. C.W.R.D. Moseley, Harmondsworth, 1983.

Theoderich, *Guide to The Holy Land*, trans. A. Stewart, New York, 1986.

Theodosius, *On the Topography of the Holy Land*, trans. J.H. Bernard, London, 1893.

Wey, W., *Itineraries to Jerusalem, 1458*, Roxburghe Club, 1857.

Whittock, M., ed., *The Pastons in Medieval Britain*, Oxford, 1993.

INDEX